Let's Talk About Diversity

Fulphil Publishing

979-8-9877411-9-1 (paperback)
979-8-9896889-4-4 (ebook)

Library of Congress Catalog Card Number: 0000-0000
Copyright © 2024 by Fulphil Publishing

All rights reserved, including the right of reproduction in any form, or by any mechanical or electronic means including photocopying or recording, or by any information storage or retrieval system, in whole or in part in any form, and in any case not without the written permission of the author and publisher.

Aditya Desai (Author)
Brandon Choi (Author)
Fulphil Students (Author)
Jamica Zion (Foreword)
Tiffany Yau (Contributor)

Copyright © 2024 Fulphil All Rights Reserved

ACKNOWLEDGEMENT

This book would not have been possible without the dedication and support of Tiffany Yau, Bonnie Chen, Maria Moore, Rowana Miller, Manya Gupta, Jenny Margolis, Laura Kaskey, Nyah Perez, Kat Lin, Kenny Lang, and Cori McGoldrick.

— Brandon Choi; Aditya Desai

TABLE OF CONTENTS

Forward | vii
Introduction | xv

LET'S TALK ABOUT DIVERSITY

    Chapter 1: ABCs of DEI | 1
    Chapter 2: DEI in Educational Institutions | 17
    Chapter 3: DEI in the Workplace | 59
    Chapter 4: DEI in Social Media & Branding | 73
    Chapter 5: DEI in Action | 99
    Chapter 6: DEI in STEM | 107
    Chapter 7: DEI & Anti-Racism Inititaves | 119
    Chapter 8: DEI & Ethnic Studies| 139

Let's Talk About Divserity Cheat Code Recap | 155
Conclusion | 159
Glossary | 161
Index | 169

FOREWORD

By Jamica Zion

Have you ever felt frustrated by the rate in which the online world seems to generate, complicate, revise, or abandon social justice buzzwords? You know, the words and concepts that come with 'points' in the social game we play (unknowingly, willingly, or not) that impact how people perceive us and the opportunities awarded? If you answered, "Yes," then this book, and the series it's a part of, should be a useful guide to our complicated social game.

I have been participating in diversity, equity, and inclusion (DEI) trainings as a participant and/or facilitator for over 15 years. I am aware of how these occasions have the potential to transform individuals, creating a ripple effect of new interactions and relationships. I am also keen on the conflict that can emerge before, during, and after these moments. One of the primary sources of these predictably unpredictable fissures are the occasions in which people find themselves "out of date." Shame and embarrassment become visible, and, usually, this is when people double down or tap out— neither of which will help us collectively win the long, tiring, 'game' that is social justice.

[A quick note on social justice as a game metaphor: this is intended to creatively and quickly connect multiple parts of the complex picture, or ecosystem, that is social life and thus social justice work. The work is hard and, while we continue to mull over problems and solutions, innumerous people continue to suffer and die. It is not my intent to reduce the significance of the work, but instead align with the tone and efficiency I find in this book.]

The first time I was formally involved in DEI work was as a young undergraduate student when I was employed by CompuGirls, an organization addressing the gender gap in technology by inviting city girls to learn programming and other computer skills, which centered on social justice projects they designed with their local communities in mind.

For a brief time I joined the forces of Cops and Kids, a program designed to teach cops about adolescent psychology and de-escalation skills while teaching youth their rights when interacting with officers. These occasions culminated in bringing the two groups together for a mediated conversation on their personal experiences and institutional or cultural insights.

One of my longest DEI appointments was as a facilitator for the Anti-Defamation League, where we went into schools and provided workshops for students and teachers on addressing bias. This ongoing professional development was one of the most impactful for me, but it is important to note that the efficacy of these sporadic trainings in schools and workplaces have been debated. These trainings should be regarded as one facet of our collective strategy; I believe these experiences are more about planting the seeds of change, and much more needs to be done to tend to the garden.

Combined with my educational background (I went to a pretty unconventional, social justice-oriented middle and high school) that includes a couple of degrees in sociology (subject areas were environmental, social psychological, cultural, and historical), these professional experiences have provided me with an awareness of the current status of this social justice game according to ordinary, everyday players.

Let's Talk About Diversity is a great book for those starting their DEI journeys, and I truly wish that this resource existed when I began this work formally. I believe it's most effective to meet people where they're at and by any means necessary. This includes not only being mindful of the content but also, just as importantly, the delivery. A lot of the first-time participants in my DEI work both verbally and nonverbally expressed that these three letters were inauspicious: ominous. Through the manner in which this book was written, collaboratively from diverse contributors and guided by Fulphil values and goals, the tone is humble, compassionate, and inviting. The authors are able to break down this framework and commitment while still encouraging the reader to think for themselves. The contributors exemplify the approach of "calling in," meaning that they privately address problematic behavior in a constructive way to educate rather than to shame.

In fact, this book will be helpful to you as you practice this method of accountability — it offers thought provoking questions, real world examples and important context, engaging hypotheticals, and plenty of concrete action ideas and tips on employing them.

One of the reasons why this book is promising is because it sheds light on individual and structural responses to bias and other threats to social justice, and it encourages us to find opportunities for progress through interpersonal interactions and organized institutional changes in every major area of life (education, work, STEM, etc). DEI work will continue to evolve as do our social contexts and realities. A lot of people burn out because it is hard to keep up with the changes but remain hopeful when it feels like there's so much loss in the game. On that note, as you begin to work through this book, I encourage you to think of other social spheres that could benefit from DEI work and the strategies we employ.

—

I haven't been pursuing careers based on DEI since I began graduate school, but I have continued to bring that knowledge and experience with me into every area of my life. Early in my graduate training, I employed my DEI background to help bring the students of my department together to examine difficult social topics with the goal of improving the quality of our personal experiences in school. I assembled a small diverse team of facilitators, and we created monthly topical programming that included short articles, videos, organized group activities, and plenty of discussion. Despite this project starting as a response to the wide consensus that we needed more opportunities to 'talk about the hard stuff' and establish ways to augment our social justice commitments and despite the consistent positive feedback from all types of graduate students, participation dwindled as the year carried on. This was an incredibly important moment in my own social justice journey. I was frustrated and confused—why was there such a discrepancy between what people said they wanted and cared about and their actual participation? After lots of reflection, conversations with my collaborators and participants, and looking into what had been written on this challenge, it struck me: so many of us are worn out, if not actually burnt out, so while we may recognize what is important and how we would like to support it, there is simply not enough energy and time to get the average person to add what feels like additional labor to their already busy and exhausting lives.

"Pleasure Activism" became my new social justice anchor, the framework that allowed me to pull myself out of a defeated, depressed state, and actually feel empowered and hopeful about motivating change in my circles again. I was formally introduced to this framework through adrienne marie brown's book, and through this anthology I had been made aware that I have been implicitly engaged in this praxis off and on for years.

Toward the end of my graduate school training, I began to rebuild my relationship to the Black American partner dances I picked up at 15, done to blues and jazz music. I never would have thought that my DEI background would come to greatly enhance my return to my dance scenes. Over the last couple of years, I've had increasing opportunities to travel to teach dance AND lead discussions or even help organize DEI-related activities at dance events. This confluence of my expertise and passions have been a pleasant surprise for me. Hopefully, this conveys the unending value of learning about and practicing DEI and that even sites of leisure, maybe even especially these recreational opportunities, need the assistance of DEI to improve the quality of experiences and the amount of people who get to enjoy them.

—

I've had the pleasure of teaching and learning from one of the authors of this book, Brandon Choi. We crossed paths through the classroom at Emory University. He enrolled both in my Social Responses to Mental Illness course and to work as an undergraduate research assistant for my projects. It became quickly apparent that I encountered an empathetic, curious, complex thinker and, needless to say, our classroom and my projects benefited greatly from his ability to connect time, place, and social issues. He raised brilliant questions and compassionately listened to his peers.

Brandon has been a role model to me and the other fortunate people who know him because of his balanced engagement in social issues—he clearly understands the impacts an individual and a group can have on an institution and society at large. A stellar example of this is his involvement in a student club called ActiveMinds, which centers on campus mental health awareness and advocacy. Just last year the group wrote a letter on the behalf of students for the college administration that highlighted areas of concern and proposals to address these issues. Of the countless students I've had the pleasure of working with during my graduate career at Emory, I am hard-pressed to think of another young adult so well equipped to write on social justice.

So, please use the following pages as a strategic playbook to help balance the game of life so that it becomes more equitable. We have been playing an unfair game, but the everyday players—you and me—can rewrite the rules so that we are no longer stuck in a zero-sum outcome. Instead of a loser for every winner, we could all win.

PREFACE

by Tiffany Yau

In a world where our societies are becoming increasingly interconnected, understanding and embracing, the concept of Diversity, Equity, and Inclusion (DEI) isn't just a "nice-to-have" — it's a must.

As we grapple with complex challenges like social disparities, systemic prejudices, and the urgent need for representation, grasping the core principles of DEI is more critical than ever. Let's Talk About Diversity, authored by Brandon Choi, Aditya Desai, and the students at Fulphil, takes on this vital mission, making these principles accessible to a diverse audience, including those in high school.

I founded Fulphil with the vision that everyone has potential to create a positive impact and the intent of empowering youth with the resources they need to inspire themselves and others around them to make a positive difference in the world — ultimately, empowering the people closest to the problems to recognize that they are closest to the solutions. The creation of this book and others in our series is a testament of this.

Each chapter is written by students who have learned from Fulphil's curriculum in their very own classrooms or have had highly relevant experiences to bring a fresh perspective to this pressing topic. They understand the unique concerns and interests of youth and have tailored this book to address their questions and curiosities about the topic of DEI—which even many working professionals are still grappling with.

I'm thrilled for Let's Talk About Diversity to bring the right voices to the table, and I know that the words within this book are relatable and relevant to our readers—anyone who has an interest in understanding the foundational concepts of DEI. I believe that the collective efforts of individuals, like our former students, have the potential to shape a more inclusive and equitable future for our communities.

Let's Talk About Diversity is an enlightening and comprehensive book that invites readers on an exciting journey to explore the multifaceted realms of DEI. It spans across pivotal areas like educational institutions, workplaces, social media, and branding, and even specialized sectors like STEM. These arenas are not only integral to our daily lives but also deeply influence our societal dynamics. Let's Talk About Diversity goes beyond the surface, offering a deep dive into how these sectors interconnect and shape our collective experience. This book serves as a valuable educational resource, equipping young readers with the fundamental knowledge they need to comprehend the societal challenges we face and the practical steps they can take to foster inclusivity. It outlines actionable and impactful approaches to championing the principles of DEI.

Like all of the books of our Impact Cheat Code Series, we welcome and encourage you to skip around and read chapters that might be most relevant to you. It is meant to be a "cheat code," and it is available for your reference at any point in time. In addition, given the nature in which Fulphil has always worked with classrooms and our belief that knowledge must be accessible, we have supplemental Powerpoints and worksheet activities located at www.fulphil.org/class-projects for any reader who is interested in sharing the content of this book in a workshop setting.

As you flip through the pages Let's Talk About Diversity, our co-authors' and my hope is that you embark on a journey of discovery and introspection. You'll learn how our educational choices, workplace cultures, online interactions, and even fields like science and technology play a role in shaping an inclusive society. Armed with this knowledge, you'll be better prepared to make informed decisions that align with the tenets of DEI. Above all, we hope reading this book will help you cultivate awareness that empowers you to be an agent of change.

Let this inspiring journey begin!

Chapter 1
The ABC's of DEI

Written by: Jenny Margolis, Aditya Desai, & Brandon Choi

All About the Basics of DEI

DEI stands for **Diversity, Equity, and Inclusion**. Each of these words represents a different aspect of the DEI acronym. After reading that, you may still be asking yourself: "What does DEI even mean?" You are definitely not alone in this question. The field of DEI was created to address the mistreatment that many marginalized groups face in our society. DEI initiatives take many different forms, some of which include educational programs such as unconscious bias awareness, or action programs to support marginalized members of your school community. Before we look at what DEI means as a whole, let's break down each piece of the DEI puzzle.

Let's Break it Down

Diversity encompasses a multitude of different identities that someone may hold. These include, but are **not limited** to, race, ethnicity, sexual orientation, gender, religious background, socioeconomic status, and disability status.[1] Holding diversity as a key value can ensure that everyone feels safe and respected regardless of what identities they hold. Diversity is an important aspect of many sectors of life in America, especially in the classroom. In a study that looked at 4,300 students in Southern California schools, it was reported that students in classrooms with higher levels of diversity also described feeling safer and less lonely.[2]

Equity focuses on "promoting justice, impartiality and fairness within the procedures, processes, and distribution of resources in **institutions** or **systems**," according to the official definition by the Extension Committee on Organization and Policy (ECOP).[3] While this may seem similar to equality, the two terms are different. Make sure to hold onto this idea, as we'll revisit this distinction shortly.

The last letter in the trusty DEI abbreviation is **inclusion**. Inclusion centers around creating a space that truly **welcomes** and **supports** individuals from **diverse** backgrounds.[4] To be a truly inclusive community, a space must not only provide support to each individual, but also ensure that everyone feels this support. Inclusion can't be reached until a space fosters both **diversity** and **equity**.

---

1   "Defining DEI: Diversity, Equity & Inclusion: University of Michigan." Diversity, Equity & Inclusion | University of Michigan. Accessed June 27, 2021. https://diversity.umich.edu/about/defining-dei/.
2   "Why Understanding Equity vs. Equality in Schools Can Help You Create an Inclusive Classroom." Waterford.org, February 25, 2021.
3   "Diversity, Equity, and Inclusion." Diversity Equity and Inclusion. Accessed June 29, 2021. https://dei.extension.org/.
4   "Diversity, Equity, and Inclusion." Diversity Equity and Inclusion. Accessed June 29, 2021. https://dei.extension.org/.

To review the basics of **DEI**, let's look at its application in a classroom. In a **diverse** classroom, students come from different backgrounds and have different experiences. To promote and celebrate diversity, some teachers institute **inclusive** teaching practices. This may look like using a variety of analogies and metaphors that can be understood regardless of cultural and socioeconomic background.[5] (Could you imagine how silly the phrase "fish out of water" would seem if you had never heard it before?) Another inclusive teaching practice is using a variety of methods to present materials.[6] This allows students to digest information in the way that comes most **naturally** to them and delivers this information in a more **equitable** manner.

Background of DEI

Every place has their own unique history of DEI and DEI practices. We will look broadly at some of the laws and events that helped to make the already diverse US a more equitable and inclusive place. Before we go any further into the background of DEI education and training, let's review some important **federal laws** that affect these areas.

Basic Laws to Know

Below are a list of key laws that have been important in the movement towards a more equitable and inclusive society.

---

5   Wheeler, Lindsey. "Diversity And Inclusive Teaching Practices In STEM." Center for Teaching Excellence. UVA, January 12, 2021.
6   "Blog: 5 January 2020."

- **Equal Pay Act of 1963** protects against the discrimination of wage based on sex.
- **Civil Rights Act of 1964** outlaws discrimination based on race, color, religion, sex, or national origin.
- **Age Discrimination in Employment Act of 1967** protects applicants and employees who are above 40 years old from discrimination in areas such as hiring, promotion, and pay.
- **Rehabilitation Act of 1973** prohibits discrimination based on disability in all programs and organizations receiving federal funding.
- **The Civil Rights Act of 1991** outlawed discrimination based on disability in places of employment and required accessible entry and exit points to public buildings.
- **Title IX section of the Education Amendments of 1972** prohibits discrimination based on sex in education programs, including sexual harassment and sexual violence.

How DEI Training Got its Start

Diversity training and education has existed in some form since the 1960s and came as a result of the **civil rights movement.**[7] The training that emerged during this time was largely focused on race-based DEI training, buttraining but has evolved throughout the years. The evolution of DEI training was often used to address the social movements at the forefront of society at the time. In the 1970s and 80s,

---

7   Vaughn, Billy E. "THE HISTORY OF DIVERSITY TRAINING & ITS PIONEERS." Diversity Officer Magazine, June 17, 2018. https://diversityofficermagazine.com/diversity-inclusion/the-history-of-diversity-training-its-pioneers/.

DEI training began to include **gender**, and in the 1990s, an emphasis on what makes a space **inclusive** emerged. This shift to inclusivity also brought attention to differences in ability, sexuality, ethnicity, and religion.[8]

Creating inclusive organizations or workplaces helps to remove barriers to productivity for every member of the organization, with particular concern for historically excluded groups.[9] Whether this space exists in the form of a classroom or a boardroom, a fully inclusive space will help **all** individuals feel welcome and perform their best. In many places, inclusive spaces are only just starting to come to fruition. With more time, investment, and access to DEI courses (like the one you're taking right now!), inclusive spaces will become more common.

Inclusive spaces are vital because they foster environments where individuals from diverse backgrounds feel valued, respected, and empowered. These spaces encourage the sharing of different perspectives, leading to richer discussions, more creative solutions, and well-rounded decision-making. Inclusivity in spaces promotes a sense of belonging and well-being, which is crucial for personal and professional development. By embracing and celebrating diversity, inclusive spaces not only enhance individual experiences but also contribute to the growth and improvement of equality and equity of the entire community or organization.

---

8   "THE HISTORY OF DIVERSITY TRAINING & ITS PIONEERS," June 17, 2018.
9   "THE HISTORY OF DIVERSITY TRAINING & ITS PIONEERS," June 17, 2018.

Contrasting Equality & Equity

While equality and equity sound very similar, their actual meanings and implications are very different. Understanding this difference is an important step in embracing the principles of DEI.

Some Simple Definitions

As we discussed above, equity highlights the need for fairness and sensitivity to barriers within a system. On the other hand, **equality** focuses more on giving everyone the same opportunities. What equality is missing is that giving everyone the exact same opportunities isn't exactly addressing the foundational issues that create inequality. Instead of providing equal **opportunities**, equity aims to provide equal **outcomes**.[10] Due to the history of marginalization in the US, some groups may need extra assistance that more privileged members of society do not need. This is where equity comes into play. By providing an emphasis on allocating opportunities where they are needed, equity levels the playing field that was previously tipped in favor of the privileged.

Putting it in Practice

Imagine you and a friend decide to open **competing** lemonade stands and see who can make the most money. Both of your stands appear to be equal: they are in the **same** location, they sell the **same**

---

10   "Equity vs. Equality: What's the Difference?: Online Public Health." GW. Master of Public Health at George Washington University , May 3, 2021. https://onlinepublichealth.gwu.edu/resources/equity-vs-equality/#:~:text=Equality%3A%20What's%20the%20Difference%3F,-November%205%2C%202020&text=Equality%20means%20each%20individual%20or,to%20reach%20an%20equal%20outcome.

product, they cost the **same** amount of money, and they are open for the **same** amount of time. The catch: your friend starts with a pre-made pitcher of lemonade, and you have to make yours from scratch. Since your friend already has a product to sell, they are a step ahead while you will have to do more to catch-up. Making this situation seemingly **equal** didn't make the situation **equitable** because your friend's initial privilege gave them a head start you did not have. This could ultimately further their outcome relative to yours.

Now let's take the lemonade stand example a step further. We'll begin in a similar way; you and a friend sell the **same** product, for the **same** price, and for the **same** amount of time. Instead of having pre-made lemonade, what we'll change is the location. Let's say you are selling your lemonade in your own neighborhood, which has a **higher** socioeconomic status, and your friend is selling in their neighborhood, which has a **lower** socioeconomic status. Even if your friend did start with the pre-made lemonade, it is likely that you will still be able to make more money selling the same product. Replacing the pre-made lemonade with socioeconomic status helps to illustrate the real-life implications of the inequities in our society.

A Popular, But Possibly Wrong, Image on Equity

While scrolling on social media, I'm sure you have seen this image or something very similar to it. While this does seem like a great way to explain equity vs. equality, it is missing a few key points.

Let's Talk About Diversity

Image by Craig Froehle

After a second look at the image, where it falls short may seem more apparent. One important detail is where the inequality is found. This image implies that the inequality is the difference in height of each person, which means the shortest person is physically less capable than their two counterparts.[11] While this simple metaphor may apply when talking about height, applying this logic to cases like standardized test performances problematically suggests that the issue lies in inherent capabilities. This harmful image is clearly untrue, so how can we fix this image?

The Image Reimagined

Paul Kittner, a writer for the blog Cultural Organizing, set out to fix the popular graphic. He created the image below.[12]

---

11 Paul Kittner. "The Problem with That Equity vs. Equality Graphic You're Using," Cultural Organizing, October 30, 2016, https://culturalorganizing.org/the-problem-with-that-equity-vs-equality-graphic/.

12 Paul Kittner , Equality vs. Equity , October 30, 2016, Cultural Organizing , October 30, 2016, https://culturalorganizing.org/the-problem-with-that-equity-vs-equality-graphic/#.

The ABC's of DEI

EQUALITY

EQUITY

In this image, Kittner addresses the problems of the fence and the uneven ground. Each additional piece symbolizes a different aspect of the equity vs. equality discussion. The height of the fence and the level of the ground illustrate the historical oppression faced by marginalized groups. The hole in the fence symbolizes the ways that many have found to work around the oppression they face.[13] Kittener admits that even his version of the image still doesn't feel complete because "nothing is being done here to address the real problem: the fence."[14] He added this additional portion of the graphic to address this final issue:

JUSTICE

---

13   Paul Kittner. "The Problem with That Equity vs. Equality Graphic You're Using," Cultural Organizing, October 30, 2016, https://culturalorganizing.org/the-problem-with-that-equity-vs-equality-graphic/.
14   Kittner, "The Problem with That Equity vs. Equality Graphic You're Using."

A few others have also taken a stab at editing the original image. The Center for Story-Based Strategy and the Interaction Institute for Social Change worked with the artist Angus Maguire to reconfigure it:

In their version, not only are equality and equity shown, but the idea of liberation is addressed as well. In this context, the idea of liberation is achieved when the systemic discrimination that marginalized communities face is no longer present in society. Along with a square devoted to liberation, they also include a fourth square that anyone is able to fill in with their own ideas. By visiting the 4th Box Toolkit website, you can add your own idea of the fourth square to their image.

Below are a few more takes on the original image to express different aspects of the equity vs. equality discussion.

Bringing it Together

Understanding the differences between **equity** and **equality** is important to properly applying DEI principles in all areas of life. The World Health Organization (WHO) — which contributes to DEI by advocating for health equity globally — works to support all individuals, irrespective of their background to access to essential health services. The WHO discusses the idea of **social equity**. Social equity is achieved once there are no more fixable or avoidable differences between individuals belonging to different identity groups. This means that the current harmful differences existing between groups of people would be solved or eliminated from our society.[15] The social component of equity is important to consider when looking at schools and workspaces. Currently, many low-income communities receive the least amount of resources even though they display the most need.[16] A study conducted by the Department of Education found that "45 percent of high-poverty schools received

---

15 "Why Understanding Equity vs. Equality in Schools Can Help You Create an Inclusive Classroom." Waterford.org, February 25, 2021. https://www.waterford.org/education/equity-vs-equality-in-education/.

16 "Equity of Opportunity." Equity of Opportunity | US Department of Education. Accessed July 5, 2021. https://www.ed.gov/equity.

less state and local funding than was typical for other schools in their district."[17] Reconsidering equity and social equity reveals how the funding system for public schools can be reconfigured.

Low-income communities are also often the most diverse. If public schools that serve diverse communities are funded more equitably, then spaces of higher education can afford resources for becoming more inclusive and welcoming to a wider range of students. In essence, by creating socially equitable solutions, we can also increase the inclusivity of many spaces.

Developing With DEI

Learning the definitions of diversity, equity, and inclusion has equipped you with a foundation for understanding how DEI initiatives exist in many sectors of our society. Throughout the remainder of this curriculum, you will learn more about what DEI looks like in the following sections:

Education:

Throughout this section, you'll learn more about what DEI looks like in the classroom. To give you a taste of what you'll learn about, here are some of the topics we will cover:
- Public vs. Private School Education
- The College Admissions Scandal
- Education Inequality

---

17 "Department of Education Equity Action Plan | US Department of Education."

The Workplace:

After learning about DEI in education, you'll move into DEI in the workplace. When you first hear "the workplace" your head might take you to the setting of a corporate office. While this is discussed in this section, it may feel different from your high school classroom, but it's not! If you have an after-school job or lend a hand at your parent's business, that's a workplace too.

Here you'll cover topics ranging from microaggressions and implicit bias to how to balance mental health.

Social Media & Brand Development:

Here you'll discover more about what DEI looks like, not only on social media but also in brand development. Many of you may already be familiar with how DEI can be represented on social media, and you might even follow some accounts that present DEI ideas. In this section, you'll learn how to fine tune your ability to spot DEI online and why it's not only important but necessary.

You'll also walk through a case study that explains how DEI can be implemented in brand development. If there are any young entrepreneurs out there, this section is for you!

STEM:

Lastly, we'll take you through what DEI looks like in STEM. STEM stands for science, technology, engineering, and mathematics. These fields have grown at a huge rate in the past few years. In this section you'll learn about the efforts and programs created to implement DEI into STEM fields and education. You'll also learn more about why DEI is so needed throughout STEM.

All of these areas represent different DEI principles and highlight the importance of DEI. As you move through the curriculum, you will learn why those in or involved with education, the workplace, social media, and STEM should value diversity, equity, and inclusion.

Ending Quiz

1. What does DEI stand for?
2. Describe one identity group in which you feel that you belong.
3. What is one of the important laws that has helped create a more inclusive and equitable United States?
4. Give an example that explains the difference between equality and equity.
5. Write out a quick idea for a DEI initiative. This can be for a space that you think could be improved through DEI principles. Some examples of a space are the classroom, the workspace, and social media.

Cheat Code Review

- DEI stands for **Diversity, Equity, and Inclusion.**
- **Diversity**: a principle that promotes a variety of identities within a group of people, such as race, ethnicity, sexual orientation, gender, religious background, socioeconomic status, disability status, etc.
- **Equity**: a principle that promotes justice, impartiality, and fairness within the procedures, processes, and distributions of resources in institutions or systems.
- **Inclusion**: a principle that welcomes and supports individuals from diverse backgrounds.
- **Equality** and **equity** are two terms that have very different implications, especially when discussing DEI!

Chapter 2
DEI in Educational Institutions

Written by: Rowana Miller, Brandon Choi, & Aditya Desai

Section I: The Nature of Educational Inequality

Despite the many controversies of politics, one thing we can all agree on is that every child deserves a quality education. Right? Well ...maybe. You've just learned about how DEI issues are present in many elements of life. While advocates across the political spectrum agree with this sentiment, the reality is that only some children are provided with a adequate education while some are even harmed by the education system. Because of how education shapes the trajectory of people's lives, this educational inequality ultimately leads to societal inequality.

Public vs. Private School: A Cost-Benefit Analysis

Let's start with a clear-cut contrast to outline who benefits most from education: public vs. private school students.

Consider the following questions:
- Which type of school leads to more successful outcomes after high school graduation?

- Who is most likely to get into elite universities?
- Who is most likely to have higher lifetime earnings?
- What are the drawbacks of attending public school?
- What are the drawbacks of attending private school?
  - In particular, do private school students make enough money in the long run in order to make up for thirteen years of K-12 private school tuition, which can be as high as $60,000 per year?

Well, let's look at some statistics.

These questions don't have straightforward answers. This first study by Solomon Admissions Consulting concludes that public school students have higher chances of getting into elite universities, while this op-ed details the private-school-to-elite-university pipeline.[18, 19] How can these two seemingly contradictory realities coexist? Well, this third study provides an explanation: it's not whether or not a school is public or private that matters in college admissions. It's the family's socioeconomic background.[20]

---

18   "Study Shows Public School Students Do Better Than Private School Students in College Admission to Top US Universities," Entrepreneur India, August 18, 2020, https://www.entrepreneur.com/en-in/news-and-trends/study-shows-public-school-students-do-better-than-private/354897.

19   James Murphy, "The Real College Admissions Scandal," Slate Magazine, June 14, 2021, https://slate.com/news-and-politics/2021/06/private-schools-competitive-college-advantage-problems.html.

20   Robin Young and Robert Pianta, "Family Income Affects Kids' Success More Than Public Vs. Private School, Study Finds | Here & Now," WBUR.org, August 27, 2018, https://www.wbur.org/hereandnow/2018/08/27/public-private-school-family-income-study.

Why does this idea resolve the contradiction?

Here's the thing: **not all public schools are created equal,** and wealthy families often end up attending the "best" public schools — the ones with the most experienced teachers, the most modern facilities, and, crucially, the most funding. So, sure, if a public school student and a private school student apply to the same elite university, maybe the public school student will be the one to get in, but that public school student is still likely to come from an upper-middle-class or a wealthy background. Students from this background make up the majority of these universities' applicants.

But there's another question here: it makes sense that private schools have more funding than public schools, but why do some public schools get more funding than others? And why is it that wealthy families always seem to wind up at the best-funded ones?

And underlying those questions is yet another one: **where do public schools get their funding?**

Do some research about that last one.

Okay, what did you find? If your research was anything like ours, you probably found that school budgets tend to be, on average, split up like this:[21]

---

21   Grace Chen, "An Overview of the Funding of Public Schools," Public School Review, June 22, 2022, https://www.publicschoolreview.com/blog/an-overview-of-the-funding-of-public-schools.

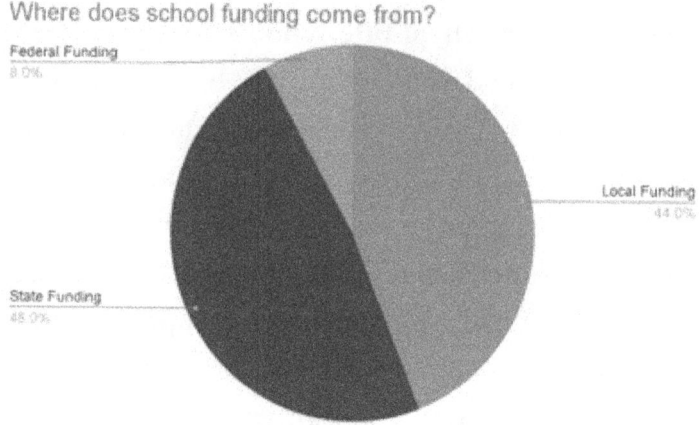

Where does school funding come from?
Federal Funding 8.0%
Local Funding 44.0%
State Funding 48.0%

But the key here is that these are national *averages*. Federal and state funding tends to be pretty much the same from school to school, but local funding varies significantly. This means that, oftentimes, two schools in neighboring districts receive the same amount in federal and state funding, but vastly different amounts in local funding. Ultimately, this results in dramatically different qualities of education. The reason why local funding varies so much is that it comes from a very specific type of tax: property tax.

Do you see where this is going?

Where are property taxes the highest? Wealthy neighborhoods, where people can afford to buy expensive homes that come with high taxes.

So, which schools are able to take in the most funding? The schools in wealthy neighborhoods.

This is why students from high-income families so frequently attend well-funded schools—regardless of if those schools are public or private. And this is why high-income families are able to provide their kids with the education that will allow them to continue to stay in the upper socioeconomic percentiles for the rest of their lives. On the flip side, that's why low-income families often have no other choice but to send their kids to inadequately funded schools, and why it's so difficult for education to serve as a vehicle of upwards socioeconomic mobility. **This is what educational inequality looks like.**

Sidebar: How does funding lead to high-quality education?

Maybe money can't buy happiness, but it sure can buy more textbooks, updated school facilities, and better-trained teachers. These are often the factors that result in better education overall. In the US, students from underfunded schools score lower on standardized tests[22], drop out at higher rates[23], and move on to higher education at lower rates.[24] This is further complicated by the fact that a disproportionate number of the students at underfunded schools are people of color and/or immigrants. It is also important to note that many states tie standardized testing to funding, which means annual achievement tests measuring student knowledge can alter the funds a school receives.[25] The end result is a self-reinforcing

---

22 "2.2 Poverty and Race: How Do Students' Backgrounds Affect Their School Performance? | ED100," n.d., https://ed100.org/lessons/poverty.

23 "Economic Impacts of Dropouts – National Dropout Prevention Center," n.d., https://dropoutprevention.org/resources/statistics/quick-facts/economic-impacts-of-dropouts/.

24 "Immediate College Enrollment Rate," nces.ed.gov, 2018, https://nces.ed.gov/programs/coe/pdf/Indicator_CPA/coe_cpa_2018_05.pdf.

25 Nesa Sasser, "How Schools Motivate Students for State Testing," The Classroom | Empowering Students in Their College Journey, November 5, 2021, https://www.theclassroom.com/schools-motivate-students-state-testing-13290.html.

feedback loop where those who benefit most from education are the ones who already have socioeconomic privilege, and those who are most likely to lack access to those benefits are the ones who already face socioeconomic marginalization.

So far, we've examined how high-income groups have more access to the benefits of education than low-income groups do.

It is also important to consider the historical context as well: the education system has been used to deliberately harm populations that are already marginalized.

Let's take a look at how the US has weaponized education:

The government doctrine defending segregation was "separate but equal," but it was quite clear that one group experienced higher-quality education than the other.[26] In Jim Crow schools in the South during the beginning of the 20th century, Black students were only taught the trades that would keep them in quasi-slavery at the bottom of the socioeconomic ladder: agriculture for boys, cooking and cleaning for girls. Even in academic schools in the North, Black schools were taught by underpaid and underqualified teachers who often lacked mastery of the skills they required to successfully teach. In Alabama, the government spent $7 per Black student in contrast with $37 per white student, and the South on the whole paid Black teachers an average of $73 per month in contrast to $118 per month for white teachers. The notion of "equality" was certainly missing.

---

26   "Jim Crow's Schools," American Federation of Teachers, August 8, 2014, https://www.aft.org/periodical/american-educator/summer-2004/jim-crows-schools.

Moreover, the very act of separating children by race caused irreparable psychological damage. When the Supreme Court ruled in 1954's Brown v. Board of Education, the landmark case in which all nine judges voted unanimously against school segregation, Chief Justice Earl Warren wrote in the majority opinion:

"To separate [Black children] from others of similar age and qualifications solely because of their race generates a feeling of inferiority as to their status in the community that may affect their hearts and minds in a way unlikely ever to be undone... Separate educational facilities are inherently unequal."

While the Supreme Court ruling legally marked the end of segregated schools, its application would come mostly through on-the-ground efforts to desegregate. Busing programs began in the late 1950s in order to transport Black students to formerly white schools in geographically distant districts, and these programs continued through 1999. However, these programs weren't entirely successful, and we still live in a country that is segregated in many ways.[27] Black students and other students of color are much more likely to attend schools in the underfunded districts we discussed above.

This contemporary form of segregation, deeply intertwined with issues of housing, economic inequality, and local policy, underscores the complex, enduring challenge of achieving true educational equity in the United States.

---

27   Gloria Browne-Marshall, "Busing Ended 20 Years Ago. Today Our Schools Are Segregated Once Again," Time, September 11, 2019, https://time.com/5673555/busing-school-segregation/.

Indigenous Americans and Assimilationist Boarding Schools

Between 1860 and 1978, about a third of Indigenous American children were forced to attend "Indian boarding schools." These schools were typically run by church officials, with the purported goal of "civilizing" the children. In reality, the schools abused the children[28] in a calculated attempt to strip them of their autonomy, dignity, and culture.

While the era of Indigenous American boarding schools has ended, the United States has not yet formally apologized or provided reparations for this injustice. Instead, much like Black Americans, Indigenous Americans have no other option but to attend the lowest-funded school districts in the country. Canada, however, (which has committed similar atrocities against its First Nations peoples) has begun to take steps to provide equitable reparations. Perhaps the US can follow the lead of its northern neighbor.

The Canadian government has undertaken significant steps to reconcile with First Nations peoples, marked by gestures such as the formal apology for the residential school system in 2008 and financial compensation for the Sixties Scoop victims in 2017. Acknowledging the historical injustices, Canada also introduced the National Day for Truth and Reconciliation in 2021, serving as a solemn reminder of the past and a commitment to a more equitable future.

Efforts like addressing the clean drinking water crisis in indigenous communities underscore the government's ongoing commitment to remedying the long-standing disparities faced by First Nations

---

28   Mary Annette Pember, "The Traumatic Legacy of Indian Boarding Schools," The Atlantic, January 6, 2022, https://www.theatlantic.com/education/archive/2019/03/traumatic-legacy-indian-boarding-schools/584293/.

peoples. These measures represent Canada's continued journey towards healing and reconciliation with its indigenous population.

Section II: Case Study—The College Admissions Scandal

A few years ago, you may have seen headlines about the nation's wealthiest families—including those of actresses Felicity Huffman and Lori Loughlin—pulling some serious strings to get their kids into elite universities. This situation has come to be known as the infamous **College Admissions Scandal.** If you're looking for a clear-cut example of how the ultra-wealthy can manipulate the opportunities of education in order to maintain their place at the top of the socioeconomic hierarchy, you won't find one much better than this.

The college admissions scandal has been documented extensively in the Netflix documentary **Operation Varsity Blues,** which we highly recommend watching to get the full picture. But we're here to give you an overview.

College coach Rick Singer was known for being really, really good at his job: getting high school seniors into the nation's most prestigious universities. No matter whether their methods are under or over the table, college coaches are an option only for those with the disposable income to pay their high hourly rates, making this a major advantage for wealthy families. But Singer peddled more than knowledge. His true tactics were an open secret among the clients who paid to hear them, but, outside of that tiny 0.01% circle, no one knew what he was really doing to achieve such excellent results.

Singer was, to put it directly, cheating his clients' kids into college.

He did this through two different pathways: **faking SAT scores** and **bribing coaches to lie about athletic recruitment.** He had methodical protocol for both of these strategies. Here's the step-by-step process he told parents to carry out in order to get fake SAT scores:

1. Get your child evaluated for a learning disability like ADHD or dyslexia. Go to a psychologist who will diagnose your child with one of these disabilities, regardless of whether the child is neurotypical or neurodivergent. The purpose of this is to grant the child extra time on the SAT.

2. When you tell the SAT administrators that your child receives extra time, the administrators will set them up to take the test alone in a room with just a proctor. Register for your child to take the test at the specific location I tell you. I will make sure that the person who proctors your child's exam is my partner, Mark Riddell.

3. Your child will take the test. Maybe they've studied for it; maybe they haven't. They might struggle with it; they might find it pretty straightforward. They'll turn in their test to Mark. Then they'll leave the room. Mark won't have seen the test before, but he's an expert test-taker and can reliably score at or close to a 1600 on any given SAT. He will correct your child's wrong answers to right ones. This is the service that you're paying for.

4. When your child sees the score, they'll think they earned it. They never have to know what Mark did.

There are almost too many ethical horrors here to discuss. In addition to the obvious (they cheated! An adult man took the test!), we'd like to call attention to one often-overlooked element of the college admissions scandal: **ableism**. Ableism is bias against, or other harm directed toward, people with disabilities. Singer's plan hinged on its first step: getting a false diagnosis of disability. **When neurotypical students masquerade as neurodivergent students in order to get access to supposed "advantages," this ends up hurting the neurodivergent students.**

In a Post-College-Admissions-Scandal world, when a student requests extra time on the SAT, there's now the question of whether that student actually needs it or whether they're trying to cheat. This creates additional obstacles for a student population that needs access to fair accommodations, as well as creates general suspicion about reports of disability—which bolsters the damaging stereotype that people with invisible disabilities are "making it up." Ethically, this falls into a similar category as a white person blackfishing[29] for likes on TikTok. When you have privilege in a certain area, it is never a good idea to pretend to belong to a marginalized group.

Okay, on to Part II of how Rick Singer shuttled wealthy children into elite universities: **bribing athletic coaches to claim that they**

---

29   By Kameron Virk And Nesta McGregor, "Blackfishing: The Women Accused of Pretending to Be Black," BBC News, December 5, 2018, https://www.bbc.com/news/newsbeat-46427180.

were recruiting those students for their sports teams. Singer used both strategies for some families and only one for others. The key difference between the SAT score falsifications and the recruitment falsifications is that it was much, much more likely that the students knew about—and were active participants in—the recruitment scams. Students would pose for photos showing them "playing their sports," the coaches would claim that they'd recruited those students, and the students' applications were immediately placed in the 'acceptance' pile.

We'd like to draw your attention to a slightly less straightforward component of the problem: **is it really that easy for athletes to get into college?** Even if you put aside the part where these particular students aren't athletes (again: this situation is clearly unethical), it's pretty controversial that the stamp of approval from an athletic coach means automatic admission to some of the most academically rigorous universities in the US.

This has been an institutional practice for many years, and it has a lot of support from those who believe in the merits of the college athletics industry. However, it has also undergone criticism from those who believe that it's unfair, both to the many other students who get rejected from these universities and to the athletes themselves. Should a strong academic candidate get turned down so that an athlete with lower grades can get admitted? Meanwhile, college athletes aren't paid for playing their sports, even though those games make millions for the coaches and universities (although that may change in the future.³⁰) So, do athletes' acceptance to these schools come at the cost of being exploited by them?

There's also the question of income level and race in athletic recruitment (yes, a lot of this comes back to income and race.) If you look at the general student body of most Ivy League schools, you won't see many Black and brown faces, but if you look at their sports teams, you will. This means that Black children—especially low-income **Black children—often view athletic recruitment as their only way to get into prestigious universities.** On one hand, college sports really do create a pathway out of poverty; on the other, this can be incredibly stressful for the students and families involved.³¹ It also raises questions about why colleges reward Black students' physical abilities in greater proportions than their intellectual ones. There's no clear answer about how colleges should consider athletics in their recruitment processes, but it's a complicated issue that deserves to be interrogated, especially by the students who are applying.

What's your opinion on the role of athletic recruitment in college admissions?

Sidebar on the SAT

Here's a short thought exercise: create short character profiles of two fictional high school juniors. One of them comes from a family

---

30   Tom Goldman, "A New Era Dawns In College Sports, As The NCAA Scrambles To Keep Up," NPR.org, June 28, 2021, https://www.npr.org/2021/06/28/1010129443/a-new-era-dawns-in-college-sports-as-the-ncaa-scrambles-to-keep-up.

31   Jon Solomon, "Survey: African-American Youth More Often Play Sports to Chase College, pro Dreams," The Aspen Institute Project Play, October 26, 2022, https://www.aspenprojectplay.org/national-youth-sport-survey/african-american-youth-more-often-play-sports-to-chase-college-pro-dreams.

in the bottom 20% of the US socioeconomic system, and one comes from the top 20%. Answer the following questions about each of your fictional students, based on what you think is most realistic for someone in each socioeconomic bracket:
- What's the highest level of education that their parents have?
- Do they have an afterschool job? Where do they work? What do they do with the money they make?
- What else do they do outside of school? Are they in any clubs? Do they have any hobbies? How much free time do they have?
- Does their high school offer guidance through the college process?

Now that you've gotten to know your two characters, turn your attention to these students' experiences with the SAT. Answer some more questions:
- Does the student have the money to take an SAT preparation class? Does the student have enough time?
    - Related: Does their high school offer SAT preparation classes, either free or paid?
- How much time (in hours per week) do they have available to study?
- Continuing to think about money and time, how many times will they be able to take the SAT?
- Who, if anyone, can the student ask for help with SAT material?

After fleshing out the two students and determining the circumstances surrounding the SAT for both of them, it's time to answer the most important question of all: **Who do you think is more likely to do better on the SAT?**

Notice that you didn't do any brainstorming about which student is naturally smarter, and who does better in school. Those are both important, but in practice, their impacts are often overshadowed by the factors you considered in this exercise. Of course, there are plenty of exceptions on both sides, but most of the time, **the people who do well on the SAT are the ones who have access, time, and money for test prep.**

That's the fundamental problem with the SAT: because all students are expected to take the test, colleges think of it as an "objective" or "standardized" measure of academic skill. But the reality is that SAT performance is so dependent on socioeconomic factors that the test doesn't show nearly as much about academic skill as it claims to convey. Wealthy people simply tend to score higher[32], and because of the complicated intersections between wealth, race, and immigration status, this also means that students from marginalized ethnic and cultural backgrounds are most likely to suffer from the impacts of wealth disparities in SAT prep.

All of this really puts into perspective what happened with SAT scores in the college admissions scandal. **The SAT is already much**

---

32   Ezekiel J. Dixon-RomÁN, Howard T. Everson, and John J. Mcardle, "Race, Poverty and SAT Scores: Modeling the Influences of Family Income on Black and White High School Students' SAT Performance," Teachers College Record: The Voice of Scholarship in Education 115, no. 4 (April 2013): 1–33, https://doi.org/10.1177/016146811311500406.

more surmountable for the wealthy—so how come they were the ones cheating?

For a case study that's supposedly just about a few hundred rich families cheating their way into elite colleges, we've covered a lot of ground here. We've discussed the institution of the SAT, athletic recruitment, disability and ableism, the role of race, and socioeconomic inequality. All of this suggests that the college admissions scandal isn't limited to a few unethical families within the tiny population at the top of the socioeconomic hierarchy. Instead, it's emblematic of the foundational issues within the college admissions process itself.

Section III: Why Should We Care?

So far, we've covered a lot about the inequalities baked into the education system—but what are the consequences of those inequalities? Sure, maybe someone from an underfunded high school won't get into a Top 10 college, but that's not the only way to be happy or successful. So how does educational inequality impact quality of life going forward?

Here's why we should care: **education is the single best way to achieve upward socioeconomic mobility in the United States.** A higher degree of education correlates with opportunities to pursue well-paying careers[33], increased quality of community resources[34], and even better health.[35]

Of course, you don't need a college degree for any of these things—but a degree significantly increases the odds that you'll be able to access them. We can look at some famous exceptions like Mark Zuckerberg, who dropped out of Harvard in order to found Facebook—but of course, we should consider that Zuckerberg came from an affluent background and likely had a safety net if his venture wasn't successful.

But we can look at a whole lot more college-educated, upper-middle-class people who are simply…doing pretty well. They work in jobs they find interesting and rewarding, live in communities with well-cared-for infrastructure, and have access to health insurance. Yes, it's clearly problematic that these bare-minimum standards of decent living are only accessible to the highly-educated—but that's a much larger societal problem. For now, let's focus on how more people can get the education that will allow them to thrive.

---

33   Michael Adam Looney Greenstone, "Education Is the Key to Better Jobs," Brookings, July 29, 2016, https://www.brookings.edu/blog/up-front/2012/09/17/education-is-the-key-to-better-jobs/.

34   "Evidence Matters: Understanding Neighborhood Effects of Concentrated Poverty | HUD USER," n.d., https://www.huduser.gov/portal/periodicals/em/winter11/highlight2.html.

35   Anna Zajacova and Elizabeth M. Lawrence, "The Relationship Between Education and Health: Reducing Disparities Through a Contextual Approach," Annual Review of Public Health 39, no. 1 (April 1, 2018): 273–89, https://doi.org/10.1146/annurev-publhealth-031816-044628.

Education, Income, and Health

It's no secret that a high level of education is associated with a high level of income, although it may be shocking just how strong that association is. Someone with a college degree is almost nine times more likely to make over $100,000 annually[36] than someone without a college degree. Spend some time with the graph below in order to fully understand the gravity of this association.

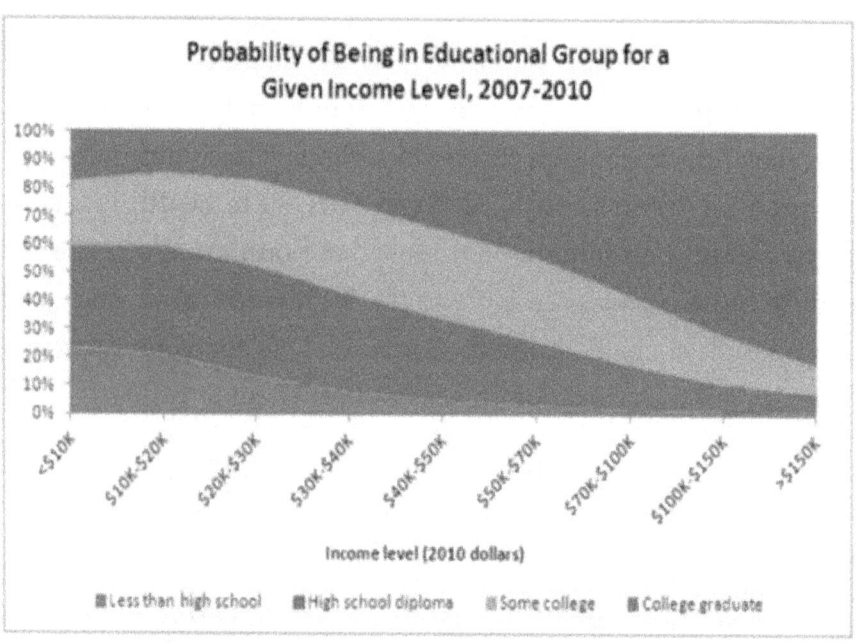

This combination of high education and high wealth is also connected to a third factor: good health. Or, rather, lack of education and wealth are associated with bad health. Brace yourself, because these are some upsetting stats:

---

36   Greenstone, "Education Is the Key to Better Jobs," July 29, 2016.

- People in the lowest income bracket (<$35,000) are often **two or three times more likely to suffer from serious health problems**, such as heart disease and diabetes, as people in the highest income bracket (>$100,000).
- People in the lowest income bracket are almost **six times more likely to experience symptoms of clinical depression** as people in the highest income bracket.
- The "federal poverty line" is an income threshold set by the U.S. government to identify the minimum level of income deemed adequate for individuals or families to afford basic necessities, such as food, housing, and healthcare. In 2023, the federal poverty line was set at $14,580 for an individual and $30,000 for a family of four. This benchmark is critical for determining eligibility for various social programs and benefits aimed at supporting low-income households.

There are a number of extremely complicated reasons as to why there's such a strong link between wealth and health, and between poverty and illness. But to list a few:
- Access to health insurance is much higher among the wealthy.[37] People without health insurance are much more likely to let illnesses go untreated because they can't afford medical care, thus leaving the illnesses to get worse and worse.
- Low-income communities, which are more likely to be communities of color, are often the areas that suffer from

---

37   "Health Insurance and Access to Care," cdc.gov, February 2017, https://www.cdc.gov/nchs/data/factsheets/factsheet_hiac.pdf.

environmental pollution.[38] As a result, people from these communities are more likely to develop respiratory problems. This phenomenon is often called environmental racism.

- People without college educations are more likely to work in physically-demanding jobs, and people with college educations are more likely to work in sedentary jobs.[39] Especially after working in a physically demanding industry for many years, the labor required for farming, factory/warehouse work, cleaning, or service work can lead to arthritis or similar ailments.

When you read about these factors, they seem simultaneously shocking and obvious. You wouldn't necessarily think that the conditions of poverty are also the conditions of illness, but when you examine the elements of day-to-day life for people who live below the poverty line, it becomes very clear why those elements lead to negative health outcomes. What other reasons can you think of to explain the correlations between education, income, and health?

---

38   "Environmental Justice & Environmental Racism – Greenaction for Health and Environmental Justice," n.d., https://greenaction.org/what-is-environmental-justice/.
39   Grant Usa Today Suneson, "What Are the 25 Lowest Paying Jobs in the US? Women Usually Hold Them," WLST, June 7, 2019, https://eu.usatoday.com/story/money/2019/04/04/25-lowest-paying-jobs-in-us-2019-includes-cooking-cleaning/39264277/.

Section IV: Two Analyses—What happens if we gloss over the issue? What happens if we level the playing field?

We've gone into a lot of depth about the ways in which inequality permeates our education system, and we've demonstrated why that matters. Now it's time to talk about solutions. What can we do to make education in the US more accessible and higher quality for all students?

Before considering that question, what if we didn't intervene, and just let things play out on their own?

It's not a totally unreasonable idea. Here are a few reasons why, historically, it has been difficult to make progress:

- Educational inequality is such a complicated and multilayered issue that **it's difficult to know where to start in addressing it**.
- Fighting against institutional problems can feel like pushing a boulder uphill, and it can get exhausting for activists and educators to keep going. (For more on **activism burnout,** search online for interviews with BLM activists.[40])
- While there are plenty of equity and equality advocates in the education system, **there are very few individuals who are in the position to make sweeping institutional change**. One great teacher can change their students' lives, but it's much less likely that they can change the whole system.

---

40   Christianna Silva, "Black Activist Burnout: 'You Can't Do This Work If You're Running On Empty,'" NPR.org, August 10, 2020, https://www.npr.org/2020/08/10/896695759/black-activist-burnout-you-can-t-do-this-work-if-you-re-running-on-empty.

- Everything is dependent on **funding**. Because schools are publicly funded, we're dependent on governments—local, state, and federal—to provide money to improve conditions in underfunded schools.

- Often, the **politicians who determine education policy aren't well-versed in the specifics of education issues.** The House of Representatives recently barred Georgia representative Marjorie Taylor-Greene from serving on the House education committee due to her history of claiming that the Parkland school shooting was staged—but 199 members of the House still voted for her to stay on the committee[41]! If that's barely enough to remove a politician from the seat of decision-making, we're in some deep trouble.

Despite these real reasons why it's difficult to make change within the education system, it's simply not an option to give up. History has given us countless examples of problems arising, politicians refusing to address them, and then festering until they're significantly more complex and overwhelming than they'd been when they first appeared. **When we ignore issues of inequality, they get worse; but when we address issues of inequality, we can solve them.**

---

41   Andrew Ujifusa, "Rep. Marjorie Taylor Greene Barred From Spot on the Education Committee," Education Week, February 8, 2021, https://www.edweek.org/policy-politics/rep-marjorie-taylor-greene-barred-from-spot-on-the-education-committee/2021/02.

Case Study: Desegregation

This was highlighted very clearly with school segregation when some cities didn't do much to desegregate while others took active steps toward integration. As we discussed in Section I, after the Supreme Court decision in *Brown v. Board of Education* in 1954, it became a priority to integrate US public schools — well, sort of.

In the 1950s and 1960s, Congress drafted federal legislation mandating cities and towns to desegregate their schools. This was a period of time when Democrats had majorities in Congress and were able to push through the agenda that they desired, despite Republicans' protests. In a piece of 1964 legislation called Public Law 88-352, Congress required the nation to dismantle the Jim Crow code that had enforced segregation in Southern schools for more than half a century.[42]

However, **these desegregation mandates didn't apply to most Northern schools**. The Northern Democrats snuck in a loophole because their constituents, while supportive of a progressive image, were often just as racist in practice.

This was the loophole: the Democrats defined desegregation as a process of countering segregation laws, and not as a process of integrating schools that simply had a high concentration of a certain race.[43] In the South, segregation was formally encoded in laws,

---

42   "Public Law 88-352," govinfo.gov, July 2, 1964, https://www.govinfo.gov/content/pkg/STATUTE-78/pdf/STATUTE-78-Pg241.pdf#page=1.
43   "The Origins of 'Antibusing' Politics: New York City Protests and Revision of the Civil Rights Act," The Gotham Center for New York City History, August 29, 2019, https://www.gothamcenter.org/blog/the-origins-of-antibusing-politics-new-york-city-protests-and-revision-of-the-civil-rights-act.

so Southern states had to institute programs in order to promote integration. But in the North, segregation was informal rather than formal. Black children lived in Black neighborhoods and attended Black schools, and white children lived in white neighborhoods and attended white schools—but that wasn't written anywhere in the legislature. While the South was mandated to desegregate through this legislation, the North didn't have to do anything at all.

Desegregation: Ignoring the Issue

On that note, let's take a look at one of those Northern cities that wasn't required to desegregate: New York City. It's known as one of the most progressive and diverse cities in the world, so surely, even without a desegregation mandate, it would have integrated its schools fairly easily, right?

Wrong. In our current day, the New York City school system is the most segregated in the country.

Yes, more segregated than anywhere in the South. Yes, more segregated than any suburbs. 75% of Black and Hispanic students in NYC attend schools that are less than 10% white.[44] Because of the intersections between race and socioeconomic class, about 75% of students of color are also low-income, and because of the way that school funding is allocated, these Black and brown schools are the most underfunded ones.[45] The result is that there are also enormous

---

44   "School Diversity in NYC," Data Team, n.d., https://council.nyc.gov/data/school-diversity-in-nyc/.

45   Jessica Gould et al., "New York's Schools Are Still The Most Segregated In The Nation: Report," June 11, 2021, https://gothamist.com/news/new-yorks-schools-are-still-the-most-segregated-in-the-nation-report.

learning disparities between white students and students of color, with white and Asian students making up most of the top 20% of NYC test-takers and Black and Hispanic students making up most of the bottom 20%.[46]

Politicians are currently struggling with the question of how to desegregate New York City.[47] This is an issue that could have been solved more than half a century ago, but that 1964 law was not carried out in good faith in NYC, and, as a result, this has become a modern issue—one that's gotten tangled in an entire half-century of immigration struggles, race relations, political movements, and urban development.

Desegregation: Addressing the Issue

Now let's compare what happened with NYC to what happened with the regions who took active steps to desegregate. Some of these regions were required by the federal government; others made the decision themselves.

The most common desegregation plans centered around **busing programs**. Busing programs were a very straightforward solution to one of the key issues with desegregation, which was that the well-funded, formerly all-white schools were often located far from Black neighborhoods. By providing school buses to transport Black children to these schools, the government significantly increased access and provided means for integration.

---

46   Gould et al., "New York's Schools Are Still The Most Segregated In The Nation: Report," June 11, 2021.

47   Eliza Shapiro, "New York Schools Are Segregated. Will the Next Mayor Change That?," The New York Times, January 29, 2021, https://www.nytimes.com/2021/01/29/nyregion/nyc-mayoral-race-school-segregation.html.

There is some debate about whether these busing programs were successful. They faced so much opposition from white politicians and families that, between 1999 and 2007, courts relinquished more and more power to mandate busing that the programs became obsolete.[48] As a political practice, busing programs have been seen as a failure because governments ultimately decided to get rid of them.

But when evaluating whether busing programs met their practical goals—integrating schools and improving learning outcomes for Black students—they succeeded astronomically. Between the 60s and the 80s, busing programs boosted high school graduation rates by 15% and reduced students' chance of living in poverty by 11%.[49] In cities like Charlotte, North Carolina, where busing programs were the norm, newspapers boasted about their "fully integrated schools." [50]

To be clear, these busing programs had their disadvantages as well. Often, the bus ride was more than an hour long, and it put an extra strain on Black students to be seen as geographic foreigners by their white peers. However, the programs have been credited with producing some of the best-educated and most successful Black

---

48   Browne-Marshall, "Busing Ended 20 Years Ago. Today Our Schools Are Segregated Once Again," September 11, 2019.

49   Matt Barnum, "Did Busing for School Integration Succeed? Here's What Research Says. - Chalkbeat: Essential Education Reporting across America," Chalkbeat, February 3, 2020, https://www.chalkbeat.org/2019/7/1/21121022/did-busing-for-school-desegregation-succeed-here-s-what-research-says.

50   Clint Smith, "The Desegregation and Resegregation of Charlotte's Schools," The New Yorker, October 3, 2016, https://www.newyorker.com/news/news-desk/the-desegregation-and-resegregation-of-charlottes-schools.

Americans in history, one of whom is current Vice President Kamala Harris.[51]

Hypothetical Analysis: Moving Forward from COVID-19

Today, we're at another turning point in education history, as our nation prepares to move on from the devastating impact the COVID-19 pandemic has had on learning. As we discussed in Section III, the pandemic exacerbated existing inequalities within our education system, and as a society we are faced with the choice to either ignore those inequalities or make a plan to remedy them.

For a moment, pretend that it's 2075 and you're writing a history textbook chapter about what the US education system did to move on from the 2020 pandemic. What do two versions of the first chapter look like? One from a version of the world where we glossed over the inequalities, and one from a version of the world where we took action to address them.

Based on your knowledge of what happened with desegregation, predict what would happen in each scenario. How does the 2075 education system end up looking in each case? Which is the 2075 you would rather live in?

---

51 Nellie Bowles, "Kamala Harris and Classmates Were Bused Across Berkeley. The Experience Changed Them.," The New York Times, July 1, 2019.

Section V: Misguided Assumptions About Solutions

So far, we've explored some ideas for solutions to issues of educational inequality. In Section III, you developed a plan for how to remedy pandemic inequality, and in Section IV, we gave some historical background on how busing was used as a strategy to integrate schools. Now we're almost ready to go into detail about other ways that we can restructure school systems in order to better serve the needs of historically disadvantaged groups.

> Hey, hey, hey, wait! You want to CATER to MINORITIES?! That's not fair to upper-middle-class white people!

Ah, look, it's the minority advantage myth, rearing its ugly head! The myth of the minority advantage is exactly what it sounds like: the idea that, by finally providing marginalized populations with the support and services that they have been denied for years, we're discriminating against the groups that have always had access to that support and services.

What are some common misguided assumptions like this?

Okay, you've probably heard this one:

DEI in Educational Institutions

> Affirmative action means that white people are getting denied spots in universities so that less-accomplished Black people can get in!

It's the argument that has existed since affirmative action was first federally mandated in the 1960s[52] in order to desegregate schools and workplaces.

In reality, affirmative action means that universities are allowed — and encouraged — to take race into account as part of the holistic picture of each applicant, as an effort to fully understand the circumstances shaping the applicant's opportunities.

Recall Section II: due to the systemic disadvantages that Black applicants have faced, Black applicants are more likely to work excessive hours while in high school in order to support their families,[53] so they don't always have the time to pursue shiny extracurriculars on their college applications in comparison to white applicants who have that time free. The same goes for discrepancies in SAT scores. Ultimately, affirmative action means that these differences do not get written off as weaknesses of individual applicants but are instead placed within an equitable social context.

---

52   "Affirmative Action," LII / Legal Information Institute, n.d., https://www.law.cornell.edu/wex/affirmative_action.

53   Cmt Admin, "High School Jobs: Impact Is Different for Whites and Minorities," Institute for Social Research, n.d., https://isr.umich.edu/news-events/news-releases/high-school-jobs-impact-is-different-for-whites-and-minorities/

Need more proof? Listen to the Supreme Court. In *Fisher v. University of Texas (2016)*,[54] white applicant Abigail Noel Fisher sued the University of Texas at Austin for not admitting her to the school, arguing that it was discriminatory for the school to use race as a factor in the "Personal Achievement Index" it calculated to determine acceptances. But the Supreme Court ruled that:

- (a) Fisher's rejection was more contingent upon her not meeting specific academic standards than upon any other factors, and
- (b) UT Austin took race into account not to discriminate but to achieve "the educational benefits that flow from student body diversity."

While the Supreme Court certainly isn't infallible, their opinions are at the very least rigorously thought through and well-researched. This opinion effectively debunked the misguided assumption that affirmative action is a way of discriminating against white people.

Let's get into another assumption, one that's often underlying the ones about affirmative action:

> It's not just getting into universities — minorities really have the advantage in everything these days, since they have all these services just for them.

---

54 "Fisher v. University of Texas at Austin, 579 US ___ (2016)," Justia Law, n.d., https://supreme.justia.com/cases/federal/us/579/14-981/.

This one is more difficult to debunk because it's so broad and unmoored. You can't cite a court case to tell someone that their convictions are wrong. But you can show them that this "minority advantage" simply does not exist. Although there are indeed many wonderful organizations and programs that provide services for minorities in education, we have yet to reach a point at which minority students receive more or higher-quality education than white students.[55, 56, 57, 58] You can look back on almost any section in this module to find evidence for that; particularly Sections I and II, where we discussed how minority students are more likely to attend underfunded schools and subsequently have the most difficulty in attaining the socioeconomic benefits of education. If minority students still wind up with significantly lower college success rates than majority students,[59] despite all these organizations designed specifically to support them, this makes it clear that the systemic disadvantages are still present.

Why Do People Believe in Minority Advantage?

A lot of the time, it's tempting to dismiss these people as racists, or as otherwise inherently malicious. *All they want is to keep their lives*

---

55   "National Indian Education Association," niea.org, n.d., https://www.niea.org/.
56   "Hispanic Scholarship Fund," n.d., https://www.hsf.net/.
57   "Job Training to Close the Opportunity Divide," Year Up, n.d., https://www.yearup.org/.
58   "UMass Boston," n.d., https://www.umb.edu/academics/vpass/aassp.
59   Andrew Howard Nichols, "Graduation Rates Don't Tell the Full Story: Racial Gaps in College Success Are Larger Than We Think," The Education Trust, January 6, 2021, https://edtrust.org/resource/graduation-rates-dont-tell-the-full-story-racial-gaps-in-college-success-are-larger-than-we-think/.

easy, and they want to preserve others' struggles in order to reduce the competition for socioeconomic success! But that's not how most of these people feel. Instead, they often believe that helping out minorities means putting down the very real hardships that they've personally experienced. Their attitude isn't, "I want others to suffer." It's more like, "Why do they get extra help when I don't? I've suffered too."

Many of these people really have suffered—just not systemically. They've experienced poverty and the many personal tragedies that go along with it, or other issues that have affected their lives and well-being. This is especially relevant to rural white Americans[60] who come from under-resourced areas with high unemployment rates,[61] high levels of opioid addiction,[62] and low levels of college attendance.[63]

When looking under the bias that seems apparent at surface level, we can see that the root of their beliefs come from a lack of education. With a patient and compassionate presentation of information, their false assumptions may be clarified.

---

60   Victor Tan Chen, "The Lonely Poverty of America's White Working Class," The Atlantic, January 17, 2016, https://www.theatlantic.com/business/archive/2016/01/white-working-class-poverty/424341/.

61   "USDA ERS - Rural Employment and Unemployment," n.d., https://www.ers.usda.gov/topics/rural-economy-population/employment-education/rural-employment-and-unemployment/.

62   Gateway Foundation, "Substance Abuse in Rural Communities," August 25, 2021, https://www.gatewayfoundation.org/addiction-blog/rural-substance-abuse/.

63   "Rural Student College Attendance Takes a Dive | BestColleges," BestColleges.com, n.d., https://www.bestcolleges.com/blog/rural-students-college-enrollment-decline/.

DEI in Educational Institutions

How to Respond to Misguided Assumptions

With all this in mind, it's often helpful to have a response in mind when someone approaches you with a misguided assumption. You may choose to remove yourself from that situation, or you may choose to educate that person. But either way, it's often an emotionally taxing experience, and you may find it easier to manage if you are prepared beforehand.

With this in mind, we recommend preparing two kinds of responses: one for when you need to leave a situation, and one for when you have the capacity to spend energy in educating someone.

For the first type of response, your goal is to get yourself out of there as quickly as possible, with your first priority being protecting yourself. So it's helpful to have a few short 'exit lines' ready to go. Depending on what feels most comfortable to you, (again, self-protection) you can be honest about why you can't talk, or you can make an excuse. Some of these lines could be:

- "I don't have the capacity to talk about this right now."
- "This isn't a good time for me to talk."
- "I disagree with what you're saying but it takes a lot of emotional energy for me to explain why, so I'm going to end this conversation, but I hope that you try to understand why I disagree and maybe reconsider your point of view."

And for the second type of response, you likely have two goals: educating the other person, yes, but doing so in the way that is least damaging to yourself. What this means is that self-protection is still a priority. That said: most of this section is about situations in which someone is making misguided assumptions about a population that you belong to. **But if you don't belong to the marginalized population that the person is making the assumption about, you can still try your best to educate as much as you possibly can!**

For example, if someone claims that affirmative action is unfair and that it gives an advantage to people of color (POC) while harming white people, you can use evidence, like the information presented above, to show how this isn't the case. Think about it like a mini essay. You have your thesis—"Actually, although it may not seem like it, affirmative action levels the playing field rather than shifting it in favor of POC"—and two or three pieces of evidence to back it up. This allows you to be **clear, sympathetic, and efficient**, that's when it's most likely to hit home.

If you think you'll be in a position to choose to educate people on the misguided assumptions we've discussed in this section, take a moment to **write yourself a script**. For each assumption discussed here, write out a short thesis to argue against it, plus a couple of bullet points of evidence.

But with all of this said: racism, and other forms of discrimination, are—as we've discussed throughout—systemic issues. This means that your responses to individuals, while definitely impactful, may not have the power to alter the societal systems at the root of the problem. Keep this in mind as you advocate for yourself and others, knowing that you are still creating lasting impact.

Section VI: Many Pathways for Solutions

Over the course of this module, we've gone into depth about what educational inequality is, the different forms it takes, how it impacts different groups in the US, and why we need to address it. All of this information is a necessary foundation for solution-building because the key to solving a problem is understanding it. But now you understand it! So it's time for the moment we've all been waiting for: let's talk solutions.

The thing about solutions is that there are infinite ways to solve any problem, and for a problem as complicated as educational inequality, this certainly applies. This can be overwhelming—how do you know where to begin? In this section, we're going to group solutions into three different key types of paths: policy-based action, entrepreneurship, and structuring schools.

Policy-Based Action

We've talked about various education policies throughout this module, including some that have been used to remedy educational disparities: court-ordered busing and affirmative action. We've seen how these policies can reduce socioeconomic disparities between majority and minority groups as well as boost historically under-supported groups' chances of gaining upward mobility through education.

Why were those policies successful? There are plenty of reasons, but we'd argue that one of the most significant ones is that **legislators pinpointed a specific problem and addressed it directly**. In the case of court-ordered busing, judges identified one concrete issue: white and Black students were still attending segregated schools even after segregation had been declared unconstitutional. They then addressed it in about the most straightforward way possible: picking up Black students and taking them directly to formerly white schools. Likewise, in the case of affirmative action, courts mandated that if a university had previously discriminated against POC in admissions, it needed to employ affirmative action policies in order to bring more POC into the institution to counter it.

Entrepreneurship

Policy changes can be slow, and sometimes one person or group recognizes a problem and believes that they can solve it. That's where entrepreneurship comes in. In the education space, most entrepreneurship takes the form of **education nonprofits:** organizations that work alongside schools and government services, often to fill in the gaps that exist.

Some nonprofits provide services that are meant to help teachers or otherwise enhance schools' work. This is Fulphil's model; we noticed that many schools lacked the resources for teaching social entrepreneurship, so we created curricula to fill this gap, then distributed these curricula to schools in order to increase learning opportunities. Similarly, another organization— the MOTH Story Slam[64]—noticed that schools rarely had storytelling curricula, so they created material to give to teachers, as well as began to offer

---

64 "The Moth | Education Program," The Moth, n.d., https://themoth.org/education

workshops in storytelling. Nonprofits like these can supplement schools' work so that these schools can provide a rich education without relying solely on government funding.

Another huge gap that we've discussed throughout this module is assistance for college access for first-generation and/or low-income (FGLI) students. Private schools and well-funded public schools often have programs that guide their students through the process of applying for college, and college-educated parents often have the knowledge and time to show their own kids what to do. However, FGLI students don't always have these resources in their schools or at home, so they're at a significant disadvantage if they want to apply to institutions of higher education. The college application process isn't intuitive, especially if you're balancing college applications with school and work.

Enter **college access nonprofits!** These nonprofits support and guide FGLI students through the application process. Some offer programs that begin earlier in high school to help students build up the academic, professional, and interpersonal skills to succeed in university environments, while others offer programs that last through college to support students through the transition and help them to thrive in their new environment.

There's a wide variety of ways that these nonprofits reach their goals, but what they share is that they've identified a specific need within the college access realm and created services to address it. Let's look at some nonprofits in detail to see how they use entrepreneurship to reach their goals.

Restructuring Schools

The last major pathway for increasing educational equity is at the heart of education itself: schools. There are two different main perspectives on what makes schools successful, and those perspectives are in direct opposition to each other. One perspective, which the federal government champions in its Common Core Standards,[65] is a country wide standardized curriculum with shared benchmarks. The other perspective is creating a flexible curriculum to fit different students' different needs.

Which perspective do you agree with more?

The answer, like all answers to seemingly black-and-white questions, is probably somewhere in the middle. National standards are important in achieving educational equality in that they ensure that all schools around the country are giving their students the skills they need to move through the world, like literacy, communication skills, the scientific method, and basic math.

Sometimes, however, these standards get so specific that they are not essential for all students to obtain a high quality education and are sometimes included at the expense of more essential principles. Do all students need to learn calculus? Maybe not. Do some students need to learn professional skills, like accounting, or soft skills, like networking, even though those schools aren't typically found in school curricula? Maybe yes.

This is why **some schools are using nonstandard school structures and curricula, which are designed to meet needs that are often left**

---

65   Common Core State Standards |," n.d., http://www.corestandards.org/.

out of K-12 learning. It's important to note that the types of students whose needs are most likely to be excluded are low-income and/or POC, which makes these innovations doubly critical.

Once again, Philadelphia is doing great in this respect — the city has a few examples of schools like this:

- Paul Robeson High School[66] is a magnet school that selects students who have been deemed to have the potential to succeed but whose circumstances haven't given them the freedom to fully enact that potential. Robeson uses a mostly traditional curriculum with various additions, like a writing class offered through the University of Pennsylvania that focuses on developing persuasive skills.

- The Workshop School[67] is centered around learning through discovery, and students design and carry out projects — like building boats to study physics — in order to gain knowledge. Starting in eleventh grade, the school also allows students to choose whether they want to join the automotive track, where they learn how to build and repair cars; the entrepreneurial track, where they learn how to found businesses and develop their unique talents into professional skills; or the college track, where they take classes at the Community College of Philadelphia, the University of Pennsylvania, and/or Drexel University so that they're prepared to enter college after graduation.

---

66   "Paul Robeson High School," n.d. https://robeson.philasd.org/.
67   "The Workshop School | Teaching Students to Change the World," n.d., https://www.workshopschool.org/.

These two structures are very different, but they both provide new approaches to the concept of a general "high school" that genuinely prepare their students for the lives ahead of them.

Cheat Code Review

- Educational inequality ultimately leads to social inequality because education is one of the biggest vehicles of upward social mobility.
- Not all public schools provide the same quality of education; the ones in wealthier neighborhoods receive more funding that enables them to provide better resources and more experienced instructors.
- Education has been historically used as a tool for oppression against marginalized populations, like Black Americans in the Jim Crow South.
- The education system has been exploited by wealthy individuals to gain an unfair advantage in college admissions; Operation Varsity Blues highlights this injustice.
- Affirmative action is an equitable form of college admissions that allows universities to take social factors such as race and class into consideration.
- Solutions to reform the education system include policy-based action, entrepreneurship, and restructuring schools.

Chapter 3
DEI in the Workplace

Written by:

Before we talk about DEI in the workplace, we need to look at history to better understand why there is a lack of DEI in the workplace. In the previous section, we discussed how American institutions—specifically, schools—often enable racism and othering, which have caused minority groups to live on the margins. Because education is an important precursor to the workplace, the diversity, or lack thereof, strongly affects this next stage of life as well. Often in the workplace, these tendencies to isolate others dissimilar to themselves are coupled with **affinity bias**:[68] the human tendency to gravitate towards people similar to oneself.

The Benefits of DEI

Now we want to articulate why exactly DEI is important in the workplace using a few studies:

---

68   Shamika Dalton, "Minimizing and Addressing Implicit Bias in the Workplace: Be Proactive, Part One | Dalton | College & Research Libraries News," October 4, 2018, https://crln.acrl.org/index.php/crlnews/article/view/17370/19151.

- The International Labour Organization 2019 global report[69]
    - Companies with more "inclusive business cultures and policies" see a 59% increase in innovation and 37% better "assessment of consumer interest and demand."
- Forrestor[70]
    - Emphasizing inclusion and belonging in the workplace leads to a 56% increase in job performance and a 50% reduction in turnover risk.
    - Long-term DEI strategies can create up to a 20% increase in organizational inclusion, which include benefits such as:
        - a 6.2% increase in on-the-job effort
        - a 5% increase in employees' intent to stay
        - a nearly 3% increase in individual employee performance
- McKinsey and Company's study[71]
    - Gender diverse teams were 25% more likely to outperform those that weren't, and culturally diverse teams were 36% more likely to be above-average profitable.

---

69   Working on a warmer - international labour organization. (n.d.). https://www.ilo.org/wcmsp5/groups/public/---dgreports/---dcomm/---publ/documents/publication/wcms_711919.pdf

70   "Forrester Reprint," n.d., https://reprints2.forrester.com/.

71   Sundiatu Dixon-Fyle et al., "Diversity Wins: How Inclusion Matters," McKinsey & Company, December 9, 2022, https://www.mckinsey.com/featured-insights/diversity-and-inclusion/diversity-wins-how-inclusion-matters.

- Kellogg Insight study[72] of 49 gender-diversity announcements by tech companies from 2014 to 2018
    - "If two companies released their diversity figures on the same day, the stock price of the company with 40 percent women would increase by one percentage point more than the stock price of a company with 30 percent women."
    - This means that shareholders not only want to increase diversity in the workplace but are also investing in companies with more diversity.

In other words, prioritizing DEI will increase the value of your organization.

Can you think of any other reasons for why DEI is important in the workplace?

Microaggressions, Implicit Bias, Harassment

Microaggressions

Microaggressions are routine insults that communicate negative messages to the target person based upon their minority identity. (Note: these remarks may be intentional or unintentional by the person committing the microaggression.)

Ex. Asking a person of color "Where are you from? ...No, where are you really from?" This statement is harmful because it sends the message that POC aren't American and will never be fully integrated

---

72   "Yes, Investors Care About Gender Diversity," Kellogg Insight, February 22, 2021, https://insight.kellogg.northwestern.edu/article/women-in-tech-finance-gender-diversity-investors.

into American society. It alienates POC from society and creates a dichotomy of "my people" and the "other."

Discrimination

Discrimination in the workplace occurs when someone is treated unfairly based on their race, gender, sexuality, religion, disability, or any other characteristic protected by **equality acts**.[73] This discrimination can be further split into two categories:

- Direct discrimination: Active differential treatment of an employee due to a characteristic.
    - Ex. Not making adjustments in the office for a disabled colleague.
- Indirect discrimination: Using blanket policies and regulations for employees, resulting in foregoing consideration of the distinct needs of current and future employees.
    - Ex. Organizing work events on days of worship.

Implicit Bias

Implicit biases reside in the subconscious and are affected by the stereotypes that society perpetuates. These biases affect us in an unconscious manner, so they occur involuntarily without intention.

Ex. Gender Bias: The preference of one gender over others. One study[74] found that both men and women interviewers preferred

---

73   "Protected Characteristics | Equality and Human Rights Commission," n.d., https://www.equalityhumanrights.com/en/equality-act/protected-characteristics

74   Rhea Steinpreis, "The Impact of Gender on the Review of the Curricula Vitae of Job Applicants and Tenure Candidates: A National Empirical Study," SpringerLink, October 1, 1999, https://link.springer.com/article/10.1023/

male job candidates. In general, a man is 1.5 times more likely[75] to be hired than a woman. It is important to note that there are also many limitations within the research that has been done up to this point. This study excludes nonbinary people—individuals who do not exclusively identify as either male or female, existing outside of the traditional gender binary—and fails to be inclusive when it attempts to address the gender divide.

How can we determine whether or not microaggressions, implicit bias, or harassment are occurring?

The Reasonable Person Standard: If a reasonable person in a similar circumstance would find the conduct to be intimidating, hostile or abusive, then harassment probably occurred. In other words, if a female employee reports harassment, and if other women would also find this conduct harassing, then there is a strong chance that it is.

Mental Health

Why do you think microaggressions and implicit bias create a negative working environment? Consider how a workplace full of these biases would negatively impact a coworker's health in the future.

As we're discussing the importance of Diversity, Equity, and Inclusion in the workplace, we have to keep in mind that a lack of DEI in the workplace doesn't just affect the work that people produce,

---

A:1018839203698?error=cookies_not_supported&code=d74d9458-f32c-465a-a3ac-cd7ff5bb440a

75   "Does Gender Bias Play a Role During an Interview?," CMS-Next POC, n.d., https://www.monster.ca/career-advice/article/gender-role-during-a-job-interview-ca.

or what the workplace environment is like. It can also have serious repercussions on workers' mental health as a whole and affect them outside of the workplace as they go about their daily lives.

DEI in Hiring Practices and the Work Environment

Hiring Practices

There are two ways we can create a more diverse hiring practice. One is to weed out the biases. We can do this by using standardized hiring processes, objective hiring criteria, a diverse set of evaluators, and structured interviews with score cards.[76]

- Create a standardized hiring process.
  - Have a rigid procedure that applies to all job applicants. This will limit subjective opinion and preferential treatment.
- Establish an objective criteria for hiring.
  - There should be an outline of the responsibilities of the job and a list of relevant skills. These criteria should not be adjusted during the hiring process to better fit a specific candidate. In order to be objective and limit implicit biases, it is important to evaluate resumes blind to specific factors such as age, race, and ethnicity.
- Have a diverse set of people in the hiring process.
  - A heterogeneous hiring team hires a 31% to 45% more diverse team than a homogeneous hiring team.

---

76   Aline Holzwarth, "How To Actually Hire For Diversity," Forbes, February 18, 2021, https://www.forbes.com/sites/alineholzwarth/2021/02/18/how-to-actually-hire-for-diversity/?sh=2dcfc96e46f9.

- Interview candidates with score cards.
  - Structured interviews may mean that applicants are asked the same questions and scored with a predetermined rubric. In addition to helping objectivity, structured interviews are also better at predicting job performance than unstructured interviews.[77]

The second method to create a more diverse hiring practice is to correct for bias. For this method, we can create specific diversity targets, hire multiple people at once, utilize targeted job platforms and outreach, and intentionally select for diversity.

- Create specific diversity targets.
  - It's vital to have a way to measure the diversity of your company in order to track how good you're doing at each stage of the hiring process. With these quantitative targets, it will be apparent where DEI initiatives need to be leveraged.
- Hire multiple people at one time.
  - This study[78] shows that people are more likely to increase group diversity when selecting multiple group members, rather than choosing candidates in isolation.
- Post job offerings on diverse platforms.

---

77   Therese Macan, "The Employment Interview: A Review of Current Studies and Directions for Future Research," Human Resource Management Review 19, no. 3 (September 2009): 203–18, https://doi.org/10.1016/j.hrmr.2009.03.006.

78   Edward H. Chang et al., "The Isolated Choice Effect and Its Implications for Gender Diversity in Organizations," Management Science 66, no. 6 (June 2020): 2752–61, https://doi.org/10.1287/mnsc.2019.3533.

- - Instead of focusing solely on employee networks, which tend to be homogeneous communities, it would be more effective to post jobs directed towards heterogeneous groups and affinity groups to attract a larger percentage of diverse candidates.
- Select for diversity during the hiring process.[79]
  - Setting numerical inclusion targets is a legal option for organizations seeking to increase diversity within its members.
  - There are some key requirements for this method, however:
    - The goal is to increase a specific group's low representation that originated from previous barriers.
    - Rigid quotas are not allowed.
    - The effort should not unduly harm member of other groups.
    - The program is temporary and has a timetable that is regularly updated.

Work Environment

Diversity includes a variety of identifiers, including gender, race, age, sexuality, disability, education, and socioeconomic standing.

Inclusion in the workplace is a necessity as it ensures that every employee is given the opportunity to thrive. Inclusive policies provide

---

[79] "Inclusion Targets: What's Legal?," ACLU of Southern California, February 26, 2019, https://www.aclusocal.org/en/inclusion-targets-whats-legal.ats-legal.

a voice to diverse members of a workforce. This is why it's important to involve both inclusion and diversity in the workplace.

Note: **there is a difference between tokenism and inclusion**. In tokenism, underrepresented groups may be in the workplace, but are not empowered to succeed and are instead exploited for the diversity label.

How to Limit Bias, Harassment, and Microaggressions in the Workplace

Reactionary Actions and Institutional Change

The ways we limit negative actions in the workplace can be categorized in two different ways. The first is reactionary action, or in the moment response. For example, as you see a coworker being harassed, these are actions that you take in the moment to support your coworker. The other type of action is institutional change. This aims to change the workplace itself in order to prohibit harassment of any kind.

Reactionary Actions
- Ex. Calling out microaggressions when they happen. This is most effective when pointing out the potential impact of comment in a calm and direct manner.
    - It may also be helpful to ask a pointed question to the person who made it, for example, "What did you mean by that comment?"

- If you aren't comfortable with directly confronting the harasser, you could also divert attention away from the harassment victim in the situation.
  - Ex. "Could you help me with ....?" or "I was thinking about our project and have some questions that I want to ask you."
  - When choosing this method, you also have the opportunity to follow up with both the victim and the person who used the microaggression afterwards.

Institutional Change examples
- Making unconscious bias[80] conscious through education and training for employees
- Creating internal discussion forums or affinity groups to understand the opinions and feelings of marginalized employee groups
- Anonymizing CVs in the talent acquisition process
- Ensuring that interview panels are diverse, and that selection is based on skills and aptitude
- Creating, defining, and maintaining a clear zero tolerance policy for harassment
  - Accurately and explicitly define harassment
  - Clearly delineate the steps one would take if harassment occurs

---

80   "Unconscious Bias in the Workplace," Allegis Group, January 3, 2020, https://www.allegisgroup.com/en-gb/insights/blog/2020/january/unconscious-bias-in-the-workplace.

- State the disciplinary measures
- Include a clause that protects employees from being penalized or reprimanded for reporting harassment

How to Increase DEI in a Company

In addition to the ideas we explored in the previous section, the following section includes a broad guideline to instill DEI in a company from the start.

- Clearly define and circulate an encouraging and pervasive stance on DEI
  - In companies that prioritize DEI, we see that DEI is important in all aspects of the company, including the company's mission, strategies, and practices.
- Specify plans and programs in support of DEI
  - Companies that truly support DEI will create plans for more diverse hiring practices or inclusive orientations. Additionally, by specifying these plans, your company can be held accountable for whether or not it truly engages in DEI.
- Have a way to measure and report on DEI performance
  - Having a means for measuring and monitoring the performance of these programs is essential to ensure they are serving their intended purpose.

LET'S TALK ABOUT DIVERSITY

Case Study

Mitsubishi Motors Manufacturing (trigger warning: sexual assault)

In the 1990s, Mitsubishi Motors Manufacturing encouraged a hostile work environment for its female employees. Male workers fondled and verbally abused the women at the Normal, Illinois company branch. Women who wanted a promotion were forced to either provide sexual favors or quit.

In 1998, Mitsubishi paid $34 million[81] to the female workers at this factory and for individual lawsuits.

Immediately after this lawsuit, Mitsubishi hired the former Secretary of Labor, Lynn Martin, to change company culture. Martin began by creating a zero-tolerance policy to help current employees.

Now, when looking at Mitsubishi's website,[82] the company promotes an anti-harassment workshop that 99% of employees attend. Their workplace reform program is clearly delineated with five different goals that the company wishes to achieve, including measures to achieve each goal. For example, Mitsubishi evaluates leadership position candidates' abilities to understand labor management and how harassment occurs in the workplace.

Unfortunately, there hasn't been a follow-up regarding how well Mitsubishi has attained their goals of promoting DEI and limiting harassment in the workplace. Although Mitsubishi has not appeared

---

81   Michelle Esq. Kaminsky, "Five Biggest Sexual Harassment Cases," LegalZoom, October 24, 2022, https://www.legalzoom.com/articles/five-biggest-sexual-harassment-cases.

82   "Mitsubishi Sustainability Report 2022," 2020. https://www.mitsubishielectric.com/en/sustainability/csr/social/labor/environment/index.html.

in the news regarding sexual assault since the 1990s case, this doesn't necessarily mean that it hasn't occurred. Many other companies that have previously dealt with the same issue also lack updated information on whether or not they have succeeded with their initiatives. As you can see, it is vital to have a way to measure and report on DEI performance.

Now you're done! You've learned an incredible amount about bias, harassment, and microaggressions. You've learned even more about how to combat these things in the workplace. This section should give you a starting point on how to consider DEI in the workplace and how to improve DEI through day-to-day actions or larger institutional change.

Cheat Code Review

- Diversity within the workplace promotes productivity.
- Microaggressions, discrimination, implicit biases, and harassment are all factors that harm DEI within the workplace.
- Diversity can be increased through hiring practices such as having a diverse hiring team, using diversity targets, and standardizing scoring to reduce biases.
- Harassment and microaggressions can be limited through reactionary actions and/or institutional change.

Chapter 4
DEI in Social Media and Branding

Written by: Laura Kaskey, Brandon Choi, & Aditya Desai

In our previous section, we talked about the value of actively promoting DEI in the workplace. We also learned about how to combat bias and discrimination and studied companies that have found success through the implementation of DEI programs. Now it's time to discuss things on a more foundational level. While it's great that companies are beginning to acknowledge and promote DEI, we want to make sure that it is no longer an afterthought! How do we do this? By making DEI a core component of our personal and corporate brands. Incorporating DEI into personal and corporate brands is crucial as it fosters a positive culture, resonates with diverse audiences, drives innovation, and positions the brand as a progressive leader in today's interconnected world.

In this module we will explore social media as a tool for elevating DEI, as well as discuss brand development and how you can build a brand around your values.

Let's Talk About Diversity

Part 1: Social Media As a Tool

When considering how to elevate DEI on a social level, individuals and companies often turn to popular virtual platforms to make their stances known and influence their following. When making these posts, **responsibility is key**.

Social media can be a great tool for those wanting to take their activism digital. One of the best things about platforms such as X (formerly Twitter), Instagram, and TikTok is that they spread messages quicker than most other forms of media. In addition to this, these platforms are becoming increasingly accessible and empowering people across the globe to create progressive change.

However, social media can easily be weaponized for positive or negative reasons. Since it is a more accessible form of media, it may be used to deceive, radicalize, or bully others. In very serious instances, these platforms are even abused in unlawful ways that may endanger peoples' lives.

Why does this happen? Unfortunately, not everyone has been educated in **media literacy**, which is the skill that helps people to evaluate forms of media and understand the point of view that the information is being written from. With this skill, internet users are better equipped to determine if the source is credible and identify possible biases.

In addition to a lack of media literacy, social media platforms utilize **algorithms** to increase engagement. You may remember how platforms like Instagram and Facebook used to put posts in chronological order. Because of algorithms, people's social media feeds favor relevancy over chronology. While this can make a user's experience more engaging, it comes at a cost. Studies show that posts triggering fear and anger draw the most attention.[83]

The repetitive nature of these posts, plus a general lack of media literacy, has quickly led to an increase in misinformation and the adoption of extremist beliefs. This harmful cycle has led to events such as the 2021 Capital Insurrection[84], the Pizzagate conspiracy[85], and countless others on both ends of the political spectrum.

With these things in mind, social media users must remember that language is incredibly impactful. Social media is a tool that must be handled with care and intent—this behavior is referred to as "netiquette".

Here are some basic guidelines you can refer to make sure that you are using netiquette when discussing DEI on social media:

- Always make sure to educate yourself before posting.
- Double check that the information you're spreading is credible.
- Be mindful of your tone. Miscommunication happens often over social media, so be proactive by using language that is clear-cut and respectful.

---

83   Max Fisher and Amanda Taub, "How Everyday Social Media Users Become Real-World Extremists," The New York Times, April 26, 2018,

84   Shelly Tan, Youjin Shin. "How One of America's Ugliest Days Unraveled inside and Outside the Capitol." The Washington Post. WP Company, January 9, 2021. https://www.washingtonpost.com/nation/interactive/2021/capitol-insurrection-visual-timeline/.

85   Kate Samuelson, "What to Know About Pizzagate, the Fake News Story With Real Consequences," Time, December 5, 2016, https://time.com/4590255/pizzagate-fake-news-what-to-know/.

- If a topic is of a more serious nature, it may be appropriate to post a content warning at the beginning of the post.
- If you are an ally, avoid centering the conversation around yourself. An important part of being an activist is learning to listen to those who are directly affected by systems of oppression.

This may seem like a lot to remember, but it's all a part of being a responsible online activist. With a little practice, netiquette will become second nature to you!

Part 2: Changemaking Accounts That Highlight DEI Issues

You may be thinking, "How can I discuss something as complex as DEI on my account?" or "What if I mess up?" Well, you're in luck!

There are already countless accounts online that use their platforms to act as changemakers in the DEI space. Through studying these accounts, we're able to get a better understanding of how to implement social media as a changemaking tool.

Some of the most recognizable names on social media are #BlackLivesMatter,[86] Human Rights Campaign,[87] and the American Civil Liberties Union.[88] These organizations and movements each

---

86   "BlackLivesMatter," n.d., https://blacklivesmatter.com/.
87   "The Human Rights Campaign," https://www.hrc.org/, n.d., https://www.hrc.org/.
88   "ACLU," American Civil Liberties Union, December 8, 2022, https://www.aclu.org/.

work to combat discrimination and have found great success in advancing their missions on social networks.

Although these organizations are separate entities from one another, they have employed similar tactics to help their causes. Whether it be Facebook, Instagram, Twitter, or TikTok, these organizations are making sure that their voices are heard all across the web. In order to gain public support they may:

- create and post helpful infographics.
- share GoFundMe pages to raise money.
- provide information on public events and petitions.
- make statements on major legislative decisions.

In addition to these major organizations and movements, there are accounts that highlight DEI in a more general way. Take for instance @impact,[89] @soyouwannatalkabout,[90] and @ardtakeaction.[91] These accounts discuss DEI in a broad sense and focus more on spreading helpful information than anything else. Pages like these have popularized the posting of easily digestible infographics that are aesthetically pleasing to users. Since they are so appealing and quick to read, the posts often go viral, being "liked" and shared across platforms.

---

89 "@impact," Instagram, n.d., https://www.instagram.com/impact/?hl=en.
90 "@soyouwannatalkabout," Instagram, n.d., https://www.instagram.com/soyouwannatalkabout/?hl=en.
91 "Anti-Racism Daily," Instagram, n.d., https://www.instagram.com/ardtakeaction/?hl=en.

By putting their information into simpler terms, the ACLU is able to explain complex topics in a way that is understandable and engaging. The ability to swipe through an infographic and scroll away having learned something seems to be incredibly popular with social media users, and many go on to share the content with their followers. It's a great way to shine a light on a multitude of issues in the DEI space and can easily be passed from person to person.

But beware! As we talked about earlier, **not all sources are good sources.** Before you share these posts with friends, go through your netiquette checklist to make sure what you're posting is accurate content. You also want to read up on the people behind these accounts and ensure that they are ethical content creators. Look at who is

---

92 "What is Cash Bail? - ACLU," Instagram, accessed July 7, 2021, https://www.instagram.com/p/CR1uTsMsnDh/.

93 "@ACLU_Nationwide," Instagram, n.d., https://www.instagram.com/aclu_nationwide/?hl=en.

running an account, where they collect their information from, and where the profits go.

And remember that, while posts like this can be great beginner's tools, they shouldn't be the beginning and end of your DEI education. Since DEI can be complex and constantly evolving, make sure to supplement your base knowledge. Whether it be through readings, videos, podcasts, or something else, never stop educating yourself!

Part 3: Making DEI Go Viral

Much of the progress that DEI initiatives have made in the 21st century can be attributed to their virality! When something goes viral on the web, it means that it has been shared by thousands (or even millions) of people. Any type of post can go viral, whether it be a news story, photograph, video, or some other kind of media.

In the past, we have seen that companies[94] can successfully launch their marketing campaigns through strategically going viral. Why is this important? It's because we've seen social movements do the same thing!

To better understand how going viral on social media can help DEI, let's look at two fairly recent examples. While both went viral, the first is a case in which the virality was brief and of a smaller magnitude. In contrast, the second case became one of the most impactful stories in recent years, garnering global attention and action.

---

94   Desere Davis, Content Writer @ SocialPlanner.io, "Marketing Campaigns That Went Viral And Why They Were Awesome," SocialPlanner.io, November 1, 2020, https://socialplanner.io/blog/marketing-campaigns-that-went-viral-and-why-they-were-awesome/

LET'S TALK ABOUT DIVERSITY

Case #1

In March of 2021, the NCAA was widely criticized after Sedona Prince, a player for the University of Oregon, posted a video calling out the organization for unequal amenities provided to the men's and women's players. Prince's video[95] was posted to both Instagram and TikTok with the caption, "It's 2021 and we are still fighting for bits and pieces of equality."

While men were given a large room with a vast variety of exercise equipment, Prince reveals that the women were only given a single stack of weights and yoga mats. Inspired by Prince, sports reporter AJ McCord posted pictures[96] of the tournament merchandise that was given to the men's and women's sides. While the women received a sparse amount of items, the men were showered with enough products to cover their hotel beds. McCord's post also showed off the differing dining situations. While the men were offered a buffet-style dining option, the women were given prepackaged meals with smaller portions. Several Twitter users also pointed out that the women's food looked less appetizing.

The video instantly went viral, amassing over seven million views in only a matter of days. The public outcry was coupled with criticism from some of the most prominent names in basketball. Players Steph Curry and Sabrina Ionescu publicly criticized the NCAA and called

---

95   S. Sedonerrr, "It's 2021 and We Are Still Fighting for Bits and Pieces of Equality. #ncaa #inequality #fightforchange," TikTok, n.d., https://www.tiktok.com/@sedonerrr/video/6941180880127888646?sender_device=pc.

96   "AJ McCord On," Twitter, March 19, 2021, https://twitter.com/AJ_McCord/status/13727591061219123 20

for immediate action. Even Vanessa Bryant, wife of the late basketball superstar Kobe Bryant, was quick to call the organization out and offer help in supplying the women with proper accommodations. As a result of the story going viral, the NCAA was quick to remediate the issue by supplying the women with the same amount of space and equipment that the men had been given.

While it's great that the issue was settled, **this viral story most importantly highlighted the unequal treatment of female athletes that continues to this day**. Although something like a weight room may seem trivial in comparison to other issues, destroying discriminatory institutions such as sexism cannot be done without addressing even the smallest disparities. This viral story, while smaller scale, exposed the inequitable practices of a multibillion dollar industry and displayed that **social media can be a valuable instrument for systemic change.**

Case #2

In May of 2020, worldwide protests erupted after a bystander video surfaced of four Minneapolis police officers utilizing excessive force tactics that resulted in the death of George Floyd, a 46-year-old Black man.

Although the COVID-19 pandemic had kept everyone inside for months, people immediately took to the streets to protest against systemic racism and police brutality. Millions of Americans in more than 150 cities called for the arrest of the officers involved and for police departments across the country to address racial profiling and ban the use of excessive force tactics. Protests were held even in other countries, in some of the largest cities in the world.

The United States had not seen such a colossal nationwide movement for racial justice since the Civil Rights Movement of the 1960s, and, **this time, citizens had something that they didn't have before—social media.**

While the nature of internet virality is often known to be brief, this movement persisted in a way that many others have not. This can partially be attributed to the continual stream of content that was being uploaded. In addition to the initial video that was shared, people were spreading resources such as reading materials for individuals to educate themselves on how to combat systemic racism and GoFundMe pages and petitions. Moreover, thousands of protestors posted photos and videos of police officers using excessive force to arrest the masses and stop the protests from happening, even if they were peaceful.

Although attitudes in the nation were divisive, meaningful change took place, and people were shown how the internet can elicit a massive response. First and foremost, the officers involved were each criminally charged. In April of 2021, former Minneapolis Police officer Derek Chauvin was found guilty on three counts and sentenced to 22.5 years in prison for the murder of George Floyd. In June of 2020, the George Floyd Justice in Policing Act[97] was passed. This act established better training practices for police officers, restricted certain law

---

97 "H.R.7120 - George Floyd Justice in Policing Act of 2020," Congress.gov, n.d., https://www.congress.gov/bill/116th-congress/house-bill/7120.

enforcement practices from being used, increased accountability for police misconduct, and more.

Now, the #BlackLivesMatter[98] movement is stronger than ever, with an incredible increase in public and even corporate support. Police departments are facing heightened standards for accountability, countless racist symbols and statues have been taken down, and education on combating racism is being supported and sought out to a degree that the US has never seen before.

While the contents of the video were tragic, the documentation of George Floyd's murder ignited a fire amongst millions of Americans to actively fight against racism and police brutality. The virality of this case worked in a way that the world has never seen before and has undoubtedly showcased the importance of social media in the DEI space.

Part 4: Crowdfunding

Although discussion and education are integral pieces of advancing DEI, we must remember that the work doesn't end there.

This is where money comes in. In order to promote DEI in a way that is both impactful and sustainable, some sort of monetary backing is usually necessary. In order to address this, people and organizations have turned to crowdfunding!

---

98 "BlackLivesMatter," n.d. https://blacklivesmatter.com/.

You may be familiar with the popular crowdfunding site, GoFundMe.[99] GoFundMe and similar platforms enable people to create a page in order to raise money for a person, organization, or cause. The lack of a set-up fee, and the intuitive layout make these pages great resources for those looking to gain support for a cause.

Like crowdfunding sites such as Kickstarter[100] and Indiegogo[101] before it, GoFundMe gives users the opportunity to tell their story, in a way that presents readers with the opportunity to show their support financially.

Crowdfunding is often praised for being a great option for those in need. Take for instance the story of 18-year-old Alondra Carmona. A high school senior, Alondra had dreams of attending Barnard College to study in their STEM program. After her mother broke her ankle in February of 2020, Alondra's college savings had to be used to pay the three months of rent that they were behind on. In an effort to still attend her dream school, Alondra set up a GoFundMe called Tuition for FGLI Hispanic Student,[102] that explained her story, setting the goal at $75,000. People instantly connected with her story. In a matter of only three months, Alondra had raised over $177,000, surpassing her goal by over $100,000! Other successful campaigns include:

---

99   "GoFundMe: #1 Fundraising Platform for Crowdfunding," n.d., https://www.gofundme.com/.
100   "Kickstarter," n.d., https://www.kickstarter.com/.
101   "Crowdfund Innovations & Support Entrepreneurs," Indiegogo, n.d., https://www.indiegogo.com/.
102   "Tuition for FGLI Hispanic Student, Organized by Alondra Carmona," gofundme.com, n.d., https://www.gofundme.com/f/tuition-for-fgli-hispanic-student.

DEI in Social Media and Branding

- → Love Army for Rohingya[103]
- → DEI Mutual Aid Fund for BAM Staff[104]
- → Trans Women of Color Solidarity Network Fund[105]

Crowdfunding has also been utilized by major organizations and movements. In December of 2018, the Time's Up Legal Defense Fund[106] was established to create a legal network for victims of sexual harassment or abuse in the workplace. The page raised $24 million, and the money has gone to help over 3,700 people. The Official George Floyd Memorial Fund[107] had the most donations a GoFundMe has ever received, raising $14.7 million from over 500,000 people.

Even though GoFundMe and other crowdfunding websites have done much to help people and causes in need, **it's important to acknowledge the shortcomings of the practice.**

Since GoFundMe is available to anyone wishing to start a fundraiser, **it can be difficult to detect if the causes are legitimate or not.** Moreover, it isn't always clear where donations are being

---

103 "LOVE ARMY FOR ROHINGYA, Organized by Jérôme Jarre," gofundme.com, n.d., https://www.gofundme.com/f/love-army-for-rohingya.
104 "DEI Mutual Aid Fund for BAM Staff, Organized by DEI Task Force," gofundme.com, n.d., https://www.gofundme.com/f/dei-mutual-aid-fund-for-bam-staff.
105 "Trans Women of Color Solidarity Network Fund, Organized by Trans Women of Color Solidarity Network," gofundme.com, n.d., https://www.gofundme.com/f/trans-women-of-color-solidarity-network-fund.
106 "TIME'S UP Legal Defense Fund, Organized by TIME'S UP Legal Defense Fund," gofundme.com, n.d., https://www.gofundme.com/f/timesup.
107 "Official George Floyd Memorial Fund, Organized by Philonise Floyd," gofundme.com, n.d., https://www.gofundme.com/f/georgefloyd.

allocated to, which may result in donors' money going to places they didn't intend for it to.

Take for example this recent case,[108] in which a couple made up a fake story about having been helped by a homeless veteran. The campaign, titled "Paying It Forward," claimed that the money would go towards helping the man with his living expenses—this was not the case. The couple and the man were able to scam donors out of $400,000, using the money for luxury experiences and items. The trio was fortunately caught and are facing the consequences, but this story is a cautionary tale to users of crowdfunding sites.

Another big issue that crowdfunding platforms encounter is a **tendency for certain campaigns to thrive while others fail.** Many of the better-performing campaigns were launched by white people with higher incomes, higher education levels, and extensive networks of friends and acquaintances to help publicize their pages. In certain cases, when a white person has started a campaign for POC (such as Chauncy's Chance[109]) the experience ended up validating their privilege in a way that set DEI issues back.

Perhaps the most serious issue brought on by these platforms is that they create an ethical dilemma. When so many people are relying on the kindness of online strangers to be able to afford medical treatment, it turns healthcare into a competition. Instead of the government being relied upon to aid its citizens, people may be expected to raise

---

108   "NY Daily News," January 22, 2021, https://www.tribpub.com/gdpr/nydailynews.com/.

109   Rachel Monroe, "GoFundMe Can Get Very Ugly," The Atlantic, January 20, 2021, https://www.theatlantic.com/magazine/archive/2019/11/gofundme-nation/598369/.

the funds themselves. This puts heightened pressure on people who are ill and takes accountability away from the government to provide basic necessities.

Overall, crowdfunding sites like GoFundMe can be an incredibly valuable tool in mobilizing and sustaining causes within the DEI space. However, it's important that we continue to look at crowdfunding critically and don't allow it to become people's only means of financial assistance.

Part 5: Activism vs. Slacktivism

For individuals and companies wishing to promote DEI on social media, it can be a good idea to observe what has already been done and identify both successes and failures.

Let's refer back to #BlackLivesMatter. As we discussed earlier, BLM has been incredibly successful in recent years through the movement's utilization of social platforms. While most social media pages have been known to show the "highlight reel" of people's lives, BLM puts a focus on **storytelling**.

Through amplifying Black voices, BLM has been able to show the **humanity behind the hashtag.** Their social media focuses more on showcasing individuals and how they've been affected by systemic racism, rather than simply "trending."

The core reason why BLM and other popular pages highlighting DEI are successful is because **they are persistent and elicit engagement**.

When a social media profile is constantly posting about the same issue, regardless of likes or views, it usually indicates to followers that they are serious about the cause. It feels authentic to them, especially when the content is thoughtful and nuanced. Including components such as infographics, links to charities, invitations to talks with experts, and information about large meetups conveys to followers that they are committed to tackling the issue on all fronts. **It shows devotion to change.**

Now, let's talk about unsuccessfully promoting DEI on social media. Have you ever heard the term **performative activism**? Also referred to as slacktivism, performative activism is when an individual or group participates in activism in order to increase their social capital, rather than their devotion to the cause.

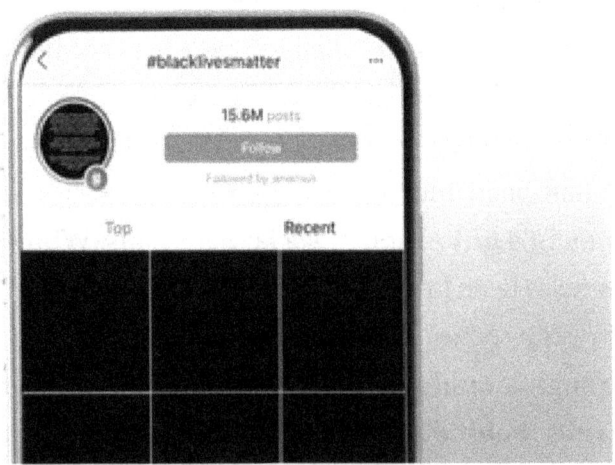

Performative activism comes in many forms. One of the most notable instances was when people began posting black squares on their Instagram pages, coupled with the hashtag #BlackoutTuesday. Although some thought it was a thoughtful way to show your opposition to racism, many of the companies that posted the squares

DEI in Social Media and Branding

had never taken steps to combat racism in or out of the workplace before. Because of this, it came off as contrived, and people criticized the sentiment for doing absolutely nothing to fight racism.

Another example of corporate slacktivism is the rainbow-washing that occurs during Pride Month. Each June, the world witnesses an excess of companies changing their company logo to reflect the rainbow of the LGBTQ+ flag. These companies will change the logo on each of their social media pages, and some even go as far as to release merchandise in a special Pride Month collection. Unfortunately, these rainbow-washing efforts do nothing to better the lives of members of the LGBTQ+ community. Many of the companies changing their logos have histories of discrimination against the community, while others have simply never used their voice to publicly denounce homophobic and transphobic rhetoric. Rainbow-washing holds a layered history that is well-worth exploring further.

It is also very harmful for companies to be profiting from Pride collections. While many of the companies creating these collections do donate to LGBTQ+ organizations, it is merely a small fraction of what they actually made from sales. This should make you think — **do these companies actually care, or are they simply turning the struggles of marginalized communities into marketing campaigns?**

Just like companies, we as individuals can be guilty of slacktivism. It is our responsibility to constantly evaluate what we are posting and ask if it is actually helpful. Social media is only a step in making DEI a part of your personal brand. In the next part of the module, we will delve into making DEI a part of your corporate brand!

Brand Development

When a company uses social media, it is telling a story. This story falls into the larger category of the company's brand. This is where Brand development comes to play. Brand development is a strategic process of creating and distinguishing your company's image, products, and services from other companies.

Brand development is an integral part of a company's identity and purpose. People care about how a brand connects to the company's mission and values.

Let's walk through a case study together to understand its importance.

Why don't we use a simple example that everyone can connect to? When you think of "Nike,"[110] the sportswear brand, what is the first thing that comes to mind? What feelings and thoughts run through your mind when you hear about their brand?

---

110   "Nike," Nike.com, n.d., https://www.nike.com/nl/.

JUST DO IT.

Everyone knows about the iconic slogan, *"Just Do It."* This slogan creates a relationship between the brand and its customers. It is both an action and can speak to anyone on the individual level. Just Do It is a phrase that everyone can relate to; the feeling of trying one's best in every situation.

This is the same for every brand out there. They need to have a strong brand value that connects to the core of what its customers care about. When we think about the roles that **Diversity, Equity, and Inclusion** play within this overarching theme, we understand that the more inclusive companies are with what they do, the stronger customers can relate to the company's values. The incorporation of DEI within one's own brand allows for the innovation and creativity within companies to shine through.

In this section, we will be looking at a specific case study, **Fly By Jing**,[111] a natural Sichuan chili sauce company founded by Jing Gao. This case study will help us analyze the importance of DEI for branding purposes and valuing a cause more than their bottom line.

Fly By Jing is a modern take on classic Sichuan soul food, bringing to life the pop-up dining experiences in China and around the world.

---

111 "Fly By Jing," Fly by Jing, n.d., https://flybyjing.com.

Let's Talk About Diversity

Part 1: Jing's Story

Jing Gao, the founder of Fly by Jing, has been exploring Chinese food as a chef for the past ten years. Jing initially did not go by the name "Jing;" she grew up in Europe and went by the name "Jenny." Despite first starting in the career field of corporate finance, Jing decided to open a restaurant when she moved back to her hometown of Sichuan. This would be the roots of what grew to become Fly By Jing. Jing believes that food can dispel stereotypes about Chinese cuisine, and she embraces her heritage's power to bring unifying flavors to the table.

Jing, who went by the name of Jenny for 25 years of her life, wanted to return to her identity and purpose. Fly by Jing was born from her search for self. Jing says, "I started an underground pop-up dining concept I named Fly By Jing: an ode to Chengdu's famous 'fly restaurants' — hole-in-the-wall eateries so good they attract people like flies, and as a nod to my birth name which I was just starting to reconnect with but still a bit uncomfortable responding to. I was beginning to peel back the layers, but there was still more work to do."

At a tech startup accelerator,[112] Jing was told by investors to solely focus on the delicious flavors of the sauce, as opposed to the story and meaning behind the project. She was told to tone down "her mission of rewriting false stereotypes and bringing diversity to natural food," as consumers would not be interested in any of the background stories that build her brand.

In an interview with Here Magazine, Jing says, "I changed my name to Jenny when I was growing up in Europe, because the kids

---

112   "Brex Journal," Brex, n.d., https://www.brex.com/journal.

there couldn't pronounce "Jing."[113] As I started to dive deeper into the food of Chengdu and my heritage, I realized that I'd been making myself smaller my whole life to try to fit into Western society. And as I started to get more vocal about the flavors that make this food so special, I started to get more vocal about my own heritage as well. A couple of years into Fly By Jing, I made the decision to step forward more as the voice and face of the brand — because it is my own highly personal expression of Sichuan cuisine, and no one else's. Reclaiming my name was a natural step in this journey of stepping into my own power. And this is why Fly By Jing is so personal — it's not just a company, it's totally entwined with my story."

Part 2: Building a Brand Around Values

Since starting her company, Jing has received comments that ranges like the following:

"$15 for chili oil? I could get this for $2 in Chinatown."

These comments sum up the exterior voice that Jing had been hearing from potential investors and white-washed natural food sections. Fighting for existence and belonging. Fly by Jing's brand is birthed on this belief that stories and cultural experiences are worth emphasizing.

Investors told her that her company's mission to amplify Chinese food was too niche and would never cross over to the mainstream (ie. make money for them). Data shows how Chinese food was the most popular cuisine in America based on the number of restaurants

---

113 The story behind fly by Jing and cult favorite hot sauce, sichuan chili crisp. Here Magazine. (n.d.). https://www.heremagazine.com/articles/fly-by-jing-chengdu-china-interview

alone. No single brand has yet risen to capture the share of mind and represent a new standard of quality.

Jing hopes to make these flavors more accessible to everyone in the US. When she first started her company, Jing knew her products wouldn't taste like anything else on the market, because they weren't made like anything else. She aspires to get closer to finding what she was looking for when she first moved to China ten years ago: a voice that was undeniably her own. Jing ended up deciding to bootstrap the business,[114] learning the ins and outs of running a direct-to-consumer[115] company.

When we take a look at Fly by Jing's branding and packaging, we start to notice that it is bolder than the traditional styles of Asian food companies. The design seeks to grab the attention of potential customers while paying homage to its heritage.

PART 3: Brand Analysis

---

114 Techopedia, "Bootstrap," Techopedia.com, February 23, 2017, https://www.techopedia.com/definition/3328/bootstrap.

115 "What Is D2C and D2C Meaning: What Is Direct to Consumer?," n.d., https://www.bluecart.com/blog/d2c-meaning.

DEI IN SOCIAL MEDIA AND BRANDING

The above series of photos[116] from Fly by Jing's Instagram (@flybyjing) tells the story of Jing's work in the culinary space and her personal background.

When you think about Fly by Jing's brand, it is clear that their strength is in their commitment to their unique cultural and personal flavors. This is the purpose of branding within companies, and this is the reason why DEI should be valued within business practices.

Global Brand Development

As we broaden our viewpoints, you might be wondering, "How does brand development play a role in large global companies?"

Let's take a look at Coca Cola's[117] brand development. Coca Cola created its own visual language, culture, and iconography to convey a bold sense of unique appeal. Coca Cola's brand utilizes its striking impression to establish itself in the minds and lives of their customers.

On the other hand, Apple[118] uses a more modest and simple design language to serve as a platform for their products. The Apple brand keeps itself more subtle so that the lifestyle, innovation, and experience of their technology can shine through. Rather than having their brand image portray specifics, Apple presents an open platform for customers to create their own personal connections to the products.

---

116   https://www.instagram.com/p/CHZB_wwhX0H/
117   "The Coca-Cola Company: Refresh the World. Make a Difference," The Coca-Cola Company, n.d., https://www.coca-colacompany.com/.
118   "Apple," n.d., https://www.apple.com/.

DEI in Social Media and Branding

These two approaches to brand development by Coca Cola and Apple differ drastically but have proven to be very effective in their own ways.

In this section, we explored how DEI influences every step of the brand development process for numerous companies. We followed the journey of Fly by Jing from the very beginning and saw how their personal story connected people with their culture and background. Finally, we touched on two major brands and saw how their brand languages were utilized to portray two very different images. It is clear that the manner in which we develop our brands holds ample opportunities for DEI to shine and guide our company.

Overall, brand development is an excellent way to incorporate a company's values into its core message and representation. As we move forward and look at further case studies that speak to how DEI and brand development work together, keep in mind what you have learned in this module. In the next section, we will be looking at ways in which existing companies have implemented DEI within their brand values. As we take a look at different companies' strategies, think about what makes their DEI stance successful.

Cheat Code Review

- Social media is a powerful tool and should be used responsibly by learning media literacy and practicing netiquette.
- Social media has served as a platform to catalyze and jumpstart social movements.
- Crowdfunding can be a great channel for individuals and organizations to receive financial support from people inside and outside of their direct communities.
- While social media has been used for positive social change, it is important to be mindful of performative activism and its harmful effects.
- Social media can be used to develop a brand's identity and communicate its story.

Chapter 5
DEI in Action

Written by: Maria Moore, Cori McGoldrick, Aditya Desai, & Brandon Choi

Our previous section was about DEI in social media and brand development. We discussed how to incorporate activism into your brand, use social media as a tool, and increase engagement through sources such as crowdfunding. We also looked at how DEI has been formed in several areas, such as education and the workplace. Now that you are familiar with the background of DEI, let's look at DEI in action! First, let's talk about what a DEI strategy is. A DEI strategy is how you plan to implement and incorporate Diversity Equity and Inclusion into your business. It is the system that you will put in place to promote DEI and make your business more welcoming to all kinds of people. This certainly seems like a complex process, so let's begin by observing some companies that have implemented successful strategies.

FS Investments[119]

FS is an investment fund company that started in 2007 with the primary goal to provide individual investors with opportunities for their money that were previously only available to large institutions or the very wealthy. They started as a small company in Philadelphia, but they now have 350 employees working across additional cities such as New York, Orlando, and Kansas City. An instrumental part of their success was their early commitment to make diversity a strong pillar of their company. To develop a plan for their strategy, they looked at places like Comcast and LinkedIn. **They took field trips to the different companies, talked to those in charge of DEI initiatives, and used what they learned to create their own model.** They set up their inclusion-council and resource groups and implemented programs such as implicit bias training and anti-harassment and discrimination training, and also began working on their civic engagement and outreach programs.

Their DEI strategy is very internally focused, with the main emphasis being inclusivity and culture. The way that they achieve this is through their **inclusion council** and employee resource groups. The **inclusion council** is a group of people from all company levels that creates DEI goals and evaluates how the rest of the DEI program performs. These goals include building a more diverse board and company, fostering a more inclusive environment, and supporting internal networks, which is where the resource groups come in.

---

119 FS Investments, "Diversity + Inclusion," June 30, 2022, https://fsinvestments.com/company/diversity-inclusion/.

DEI IN ACTION

The **resource groups** provide professional development opportunities, create charitable and professional partnerships with outside organizations, and recruit from new colleges. They also offer more expertise when the company is making DEI-related decisions. Their six different groups are as follows:

- FS Heroes: This group helps veterans who work at the company and in the industry.
- FS in Color: This group focuses on POC. They do the same work as FS Heroes, and they also help students look into the financial field.
- FS Pride: This group fosters an inclusive environment for all employees and clients to be their authentic selves.
- FS Women's Network: This group committed to the advancement of women in the financial field.
- FS Family Network: This group helps employees with families maintain a healthy work-life balance.

While they are focused on the inner side of DEI, FS Investments also has an excellent external program beyond just donating to charities. This includes their employees' service requirement and their promotion of equity in the field of finance. **They created a program called Philadelphia Financial Scholars that works with the University of Pennsylvania to teach financial literacy to high school students and their families.** They have three different programs, which are as follows:

- Financial education: this program teaches students how to make smart financial decisions, budget, and save for the future.

- Entrepreneur incubator: this after-school program teaches students the entrepreneurial mindset and how to apply it.
- Financial education for parents and caretakers: this program teaches adults skills like smart shopping, saving for life events, and introducing them to investing.

Case Study: Bimbo Bakeries USA[120]

Bimbo Bakeries is an international baking company. Its headquarters are in Mexico, but we will focus on the branch here in the US. Bimbo Bakeries USA has 60 bakeries, over 20,000 employees, and 21 brands that distribute baked goods all across the country. They started their DEI journey in 2020, appointing Nikki Lang as their first Head of DEI. Since then, they have been very focused on both the internal and external aspects of DEI within the organization. Because they operate on such a large scale, creating an internal culture that leads to external change is difficult, but the DEI team at BBU does an excellent job in making this possible. Here is how they did it.

BBU started their DEI journey in 2020 with the creation of the **Racial Equity Action Council.** The goal of this council was to help renew people's practices in the company. The first way that they did this was by creating a business inclusion group that focused on Black associates and more diverse community and supplier relationships.

The action council is not all that BBU is doing. The rest of the internal strategy consists of things like policy work and upholding the company's values. While the policy work sounds like signing

---

[120] "BimboBakeries," Bimbo Bakeries USA, n.d., https://www.bimbobakeriesusa.com/.

papers, a lot more goes into it. Policy work covers areas ranging from commercial re-shoots that focus on a more diverse cast to guidelines and benefits for those on parental leave. All of this important work requires **close communication with staff and making sure that they all feel heard.**

The Values of the Company

BBU has three different values that they honor through their policies and practices. These values have also enacted some new approaches. They are as follows:

- The first is that BBU **values the person.** This value goes hand-in-hand with their "#youbelong" campaign. These respect the fact that the employees are individuals who deserve respect and autonomy in their choices.
- The next value is all about the **workforce**. Their goal here is to create one that is more inclusive and representative. Ultimately, this is to make people feel like they belong their place of work.
- The last value teaches people to understand that **everyone is different and should be treated with respect and kindness**. There is one other practice that is important at BBU, which is cultural celebrations. These are company-wide celebrations of things like Black History Month, Women's History Month, Pride Month, and Latino History Month. This practice, in particular, has gone over well with the employees in the company.

BBU's external side of their program has two ways of reaching out to all of the communities they are a part of. **The first is in the**

marketplace. In this business area, they look for partners that invest back into the communities they are in. In what ways do these partners support the community?

The second is donations. They have many different places where they donate, such as the United Negro College Fund, which is their national partner. This organization funds the education of Black students and finds them opportunities like scholarships and internships. In the east, BBU has partnered with the Philadelphia school district and rebel ventures. In the Southeast, the organization is partnered with 100 Black women of Atlanta. In Chicago, they are partnered with Insertion Corp. and Chicago scholars. In the West, they are partnered with 100 Black men from the Bay Area. Because BBU exists on such a big scale, setting up a strong DEI program could be challenging but their efforts have resulted in positive impacts across the country.

Coded by Kids[121]

Coded by Kids is a **non-profit that teaches kids how to code, and it was founded on a DEI strategy.** The CEO and founder, Sylvester Mobley, worked in the tech industry for many years but became frustrated with the lack of diversity in the field. On their website, they give background on the issues. For racial inequality, they reference that "by 2030, the employment outlook for African Americans-particularly men, younger workers (ages 18-35), and those without a college degree-may worsen dramatically." For gender inequality, that same consulting firm found that "the percentage of computing

---

[121] Coded By Kids, "Coded by Kids," n.d., https://codedbykids.com/.

roles women hold has largely declined in the United States over the past 25 years." These two statistics show how drastic the issues are.

The goal of Coded by Kids is to help those underrepresented populations get more opportunities in the tech field. They also aim to get kids excited about coding and technology to introduce more diversity into the field.

Their founder began by teaching kids how to code in a local recreation center. The number of students he had started to increase, and Coded by Kids became an official organization in 2014. As of 2019, almost 700 students have taken classes with them. They have 12 full-time employees and teach in centers and schools in Philadelphia, Delaware, and New Jersey. What makes them different from other coding schools is that they prioritize social impact over profits. Their commitment to developing opportunities and representation is helping students from historically marginalized communities into better futures, as well as increasing diversity in STEM fields.

There are many ways to include DEI in your company, and there are many different strategies and methods that you can use. It also doesn't matter the company's size; even if it is small, there are various ways that your organization can practice DEI:

- Make culture your priority.
- Focus on equity both in and out of your business.
- Make DEI the focus of your company culture.
- Donate to places and make sure that your connection and partners align with your company's values.

Cheat Code Review

- DEI strategies are plans aimed to guide businesses and organizations in promoting DEI principles so that they can be more welcoming to all individuals.

Chapter 6
DEI in STEM

Written by: Manya Gupta, Aditya Desai, & Brandon Choi

After reading the previous section, hopefully you began thinking more about how to implement DEI in a company setting. Now that you've learned about that aspect, let's look at DEI in a specific field: STEM!

Now I'm sure you've all heard this before, but STEM stands for Science, Technology, Engineering, and Mathematics. Pretty cool, right? There are so many fields in STEM! Computer science, astronomy, chemistry—it goes on and on. Almost every profession has a STEM aspect connected to it, and that's why it's so important that we learn about it. In this module, we will explore minority representation in STEM, how it has evolved throughout the years, and how we can make STEM a more inclusive field.

STEM education gives students the skills to solve some of the world's most important problems, ranging from climate change to public health. **As our world becomes more centralized on technology, STEM education is effective to provide quantitative reasoning skills such as coding and critical thinking.**

For example: climate change, one of our most time-sensitive issues, can be mitigated with new innovations—electric cars, improved transportation systems, sustainable architecture, etc. We need specialized workers to make this happen, such as climatologists and engineers. Can you guess which field these individuals come from? You got it, STEM!

That's why it's so important that we have diversity, equity, and inclusion in this field. DEI leads to better STEM performance. **Having diverse perspectives is a strength because each individual takes a different approach to solving issues.** Think about the following scenario: There are 20 people in a room, and they split off into two groups of 10. But, Group 1 has far more diversity: these 10 people come from different races, socioeconomic classes, and backgrounds, while Group 2 is composed of individuals from similar environments. Which group do you think will (most likely) have the greatest potential? If you guessed Group 1, then you're correct!

Why?

Every person can draw from their own experiences to identify problems and create solutions. If they all have similar experiences, they will probably all construct variations of the same solution. On the other hand, individuals from diverse backgrounds can come together and bring in a more dynamic range of thought and problem-solving.

Studies[122] have shown that diverse teams have outperformed less diverse ones, even if the latter is considered to be more skilled.

Either way, chances are that you haven't seen or found as much diversity as you would have liked. So this begs the question: has it always been this way?

---

122   Lu Hong and Scott E. Page, "Groups of Diverse Problem Solvers Can Outperform Groups of High-Ability Problem Solvers," Proceedings of the National Academy of Sciences 101, no. 46 (November 8, 2004): 16385–89, https://doi.org/10.1073/pnas.0403723101.

Minorities in STEM Throughout the Years

Unfortunately, it seems so. Statistically, diversity in STEM hasn't increased in the past two decades. Two decades! What's even more interesting is that POC representation increased 24% in the workforce from 2001-2015, which is a big jump. However, POC representation in STEM saw no increase at all.

Why is that the case? Let's explore the root of the problem. As we learned in the DEI in the education section, schools with a high percentage of minority students often don't have as many resources available to them as their counterparts. Such schools are often underfunded because funding comes down to the wealth of the area and how much people pay in taxes. If the school is situated in a heavily minority area, then it is possible that that area does not have as much wealth as predominantly white areas.

These schools also may not offer as many higher-level STEM classes. They may not have as many enrichment programs outside of school as well. Do you see the pattern? Minority-identifying kids can't cultivate a love for the STEM field if they aren't adequately exposed to it.

Another reason why minority students are not represented in STEM is that they are sometimes stuck in a cyclical pattern of not having access to resources. This sounds confusing, but it's not! Let's look at this in terms of an example.

Imagine one child is currently going to school. They want to get some extra math material from their parents to help them study, but the problem is that their parents didn't have these resources themselves growing up (this could be for a number of reasons). So, they are having trouble giving them to their kids. Because of this, the child may grow up and be in the same position.

Since they did not get the extra math materials from their parents, they may not give extra math materials to their own future kids—that's why it's so hard to fix the problem. The cycle keeps going on and on, until someone is fortunate enough to break out of it. What's even worse is that the further the cycle goes on, the more the conflict perpetuates in these communities.

So do you see what happens? Now, we are by no means saying that any of this affects all minority-identifying students or families! But it unfortunately happens to some.

Now, we know what you must be thinking. There are so many programs out there for kids to get involved in STEM! Why don't they try these programs? Well...that's true. Outreach efforts and programs, especially online, have increased greatly. There are so many more of them now than there were 15 years ago. But still, there hasn't been an increase in STEM representation in the workforce.

Black Americans comprised nine percent of the STEM workforce in 2016,[123] and that number stayed stagnant through 2019. Over the same time period, Hispanic representation only rose from 7-8%. Again, the main culprit of these staggering numbers is the lack of educational opportunities. They show us that we still have a long way to go in terms of education.

---

123   Fry, R. (2021, April 1). Stem jobs see uneven progress in increasing gender, racial and ethnic diversity. Pew Research Center Science & Society. https://www.pewresearch.org/science/2021/04/01/stem-jobs-see-uneven-progress-in-increasing-gender-racial-and-ethnic-diversity/

STEM Opportunities

We do have a lot to do, but as we mentioned earlier, there are opportunities for minority students to get involved in STEM activities.

First off, the easiest way to get involved is to participate in STEM classes and clubs. But again, some schools don't have many to offer. So what else can students do?

1. **Online and In-Person Contests**

There are several online and in-person STEM contests available to minority students, especially those who are high schoolers. Take for instance the Modeling the Future Challenge![124] This is a competition for high school math students that would like to win a college scholarship. As part of the competition, students must answer questions and submit a project proposal.

Another competition available to students is the TEAMS competition. TEAMS[125] stands for Tests of Engineering Aptitude, Mathematics, and Science, and is available to all middle and high schoolers. The event includes multiple choice questions, essays, and a building component!

Unfortunately, such competitions can present certain challenges. One of them is registration fees. Countless STEM competitions have fees which students need to pay in order to enter—for example, the TEAMS competition has a fee of $150! An amount like this could

---

124 "Modeling the Future Challenge – Real-World Actuarial Math Modeling Scholarship Competition for High School Students!," n.d., https://www.mtfchallenge.org/.
125 "TEAMS," n.d., https://tsaweb.org/teams.

be very difficult to obtain for many underprivileged families. Other competitions that you may have heard of that include registration fees are HOSA, The Conrad Challenge, and Academic Decathlon.

Second, sometimes your school needs to get official recognition in order to get you or your team registered. This can be a lengthy process, especially if you need administration approval.

Finally, should you or your team make it to the state or national level, you may have to account for travel costs if your school doesn't cover them. It may be damaging to your morale if you advance to high levels but are not able to compete because of finances. Oftentimes, these costs disproportionately affect low-income students, many of which are POC. However, some competitions, such as the Conrad Challenge, offer merit and need-based scholarships!

2. **Specialized Research Programs**

Now that we've gone over the competitions, let's get into programs. There are a few research programs, especially for students of color. There are different types of research programs, but oftentimes students in the program (by themselves or in a group) research an assigned topic or one of their choice. Then, they produce a final product, which is often a paper. An example of a research program is Talaria. Talaria[126] is a free research program specifically geared towards low income or minority students. Each student will be paired with a mentor when writing a research paper on the topic of their choice!

---

126 "Talaria Summer Institute," Talaria ATHENA, n.d., https://talariasummerinstitute.org/.

DEI in STEM

3. Specialized Organizations

Finally, there are designated organizations for students of color too! One such organization is Black Girls Code. As the name suggests, Black Girls Code[127] is an organization devoted to teaching Black girls coding and other computer science skills.

Even though these programs and organizations exist, there are disparities between them and other non-specialized organizations. For example, minority-oriented organizations often don't receive as much funding as others—nor do they receive as much publicity.

So, the moral of the story is that we could do better in offering more STEM opportunities to students of color hoping to enter the field. That being said, students can take advantage of the ones that are out there. We only mentioned a couple—with a bit of research, you can find so many more!

Ways to Promote DEI in STEM

Now that we've gone over what STEM opportunities are available to students, let's go over a few ways that students, schools, and employers can promote diversity, equity, and inclusion in STEM.

1. Establish Diversity Offices

One way to promote DEI in classrooms is to establish diversity offices within schools. Diversity offices are places for minority-identifying students to acquire educational resources and counseling at their high school, or especially their university. These offices

---

127   Black Girls CODE, "BGC," November 19, 2022, https://wearebgc.org/.

provide a great place for students to find opportunities and pursue their college degrees.

For example, the Multicultural Resource Center at Penn State University[128] is a central place for students of color that provides more than just educational resources. MRC staff work with students on topics such as university regulations, internships, test-taking strategies, scholarships/financial aid, and bias-motivated incidents.

2. **Offer more STEM Courses**

As we've been saying, STEM courses need to be offered in high schools and colleges with a high minority population! Higher level classes such as AP classes should also be offered.

3. **Increase Financial Aid Opportunities**

Financial aid opportunities are often vital for students that want to pursue higher education. If additional financial aid opportunities were available to them, then more students could pursue STEM majors! This would allow for added diversity in college STEM classes and workplaces.

4. **Reform College Admissions Advertisement**

Colleges can also place extra focus on recruiting and maintaining underrepresented populations. Oftentimes, college outreach does not reach minority or low-income communities, so students don't know about their chances to attend that school or the financial aid they'll

---

128 "Multicultural Resource Center (MRC)— Office of the Vice Provost for Educational Equity," n.d., http://equity.psu.edu/mrc.

receive if they do. Colleges can do a better job of communicating this information so they can reach more POC students!

But once colleges admit those students, they must also take measures to ensure they are being thoroughly supported. To do so, colleges can set up the previously mentioned diversity offices and implement a mentorship program.

5. Increase Awareness of Existing STEM Opportunities

Finally, teachers, staff, and opportunity organizers should highlight the STEM opportunities that are out there. This helps the programs reach their intended target while broadening the perspective of students.

As a student yourself, implementing some of these changes may feel out of reach. However, you can advocate for these adjustments in your school by speaking with your school's administration and sharing these ideas with your peers.

Case Studies

To conclude our section on DEI in STEM, we'll turn the spotlight to minority individuals who paved their pathway through their work in the STEM field.

Our first example is Dr. Ellen Ochoa. Dr. Ellen Ochoa is a former NASA astronaut and the former director of the Johnson Space Center. In fact, she was the first Hispanic woman to go to space! However, she did not reach this point without encountering challenges.

Despite continuously being one of the only women in many of her classes and jobs, she persisted and remained in the STEM field. Her strong foundation of STEM classes in high school and college contributed to her success. When she graduated from college, she went into the optics field. Her research and accomplishments gained her the attention of NASA, and she was admitted to their astronaut training program. As she went through this process, she drew support from the Hispanic community and role models such as Sally Ride (the first American woman in space).

From there, she went on to travel on four space missions and rose through the ranks to become the director of the Johnson Space Center. **Ellen Ochoa paved her way through persistence and by taking advantage of the opportunities put before her.**

The second woman we want to highlight is Kimberly Bryant. She paved her pathway within STEM from a community perspective and by empowering those around her.

Kimberly Bryant was an electrical engineer before she became an advocate for a more inclusive STEM world. She also held jobs related to biotechnology and pharmaceuticals. Her experience was similar to Ellen Ochoa's—she was struck by the lack of representation in her STEM classes and work environment. When her daughter Kai expressed an interest in computer science, Bryant saw that not much had changed since she was young. There were still very minimal amounts of representation in STEM classes and programs! All the programs she could find for her daughter were not very diverse. This predicament revealed the lack of change in minority opportunities and representation throughout the years, but Bryant decided to do something about it.

She founded Black Girls Code, a nonprofit organization devoted to teaching Black American girls coding and other computer-related skills. **She paved her path through advocacy and action,** striving to ensure that no other Black American girls would experience the disparity in STEM opportunities the same way she did.

Now that you've learned all about DEI in STEM, it's time to take action. What can you do to make a difference? Hopefully we have given you a foundation to go forward and create change in the STEM world. It's up to each and every one of you—so get yourselves out there. We can't wait to see what you accomplish!

Cheat Code Review

- The STEM fields are playing crucial roles in shaping current and future societies, so it is important that they are composed of diverse individuals.
- Minority representation in STEM is slow to increase, but numerous individuals and organizations are stepping up to increase awareness and provide opportunities.
- Methods to promoting diversity within STEM include establishing diversity offices, increasing course offerings in diverse schools, increasing financial aid opportunities, reforming college recruitment, and increasing awareness of existing opportunities.

Chapter 7
DEI and Anti-Racism Initiatives

Written by: Bonnie Chen, Cori McGoldrick, & Aditya Desai

Section I: Historical Racism in the US

First, let's start with some simple definitions. Like we have previously discussed, equality and equity are not the same. Similarly, there is a key difference between the terms **systematic**, and **systemic**, that is important to understand in the context of racial injustice.

- **Systematic**: An action that is consistently repeated. For example, "She systematically watered her plant every two weeks, as instructed."
- **Systemic**: Affecting the entire system, not just one part. For example, "It's good the leak wasn't systemic, it's localized to a particular engine."

What Does This Mean?
Under the backdrop of American history, we can begin to understand why these words matter. Many people claim that racism is a relic: something done by individuals (systematic racism) instead of acknowledging their enablement of a deeply flawed system (systemic racism).

The rhetoric that racism is systematic, rather than systemic, is a harmful **myth**. This often is a **feel-good solution:** it alleviates individuals of guilt and settles their conscience, allowing them to believe that as long as they don't perpetuate racism, they are not the problem.

This ultimately **avoids accountability**, and worse, the drive to dismantle a system that was created to protect and maintain white supremacy and wealth during a time when POC and women were property and second-class citizens.

Instead, we look at working *together* to actively challenge aspects of systemic racism that hinder societal growth.

Section II: How Does Systemic Racism Work?

Let's take a look at this graph from the United States Census Bureau.[129]

---

129   US Census Bureau, "Inequalities Persist Despite Decline in Poverty For All Major Race and Hispanic Origin Groups," Census.gov, December 9, 2021, https://www.census.gov/library/stories/2020/09/poverty-rates-for-blacks-and-hispanics-reached-historic-lows-in-2019.html.

DEI and Anti-Racism Initiatives

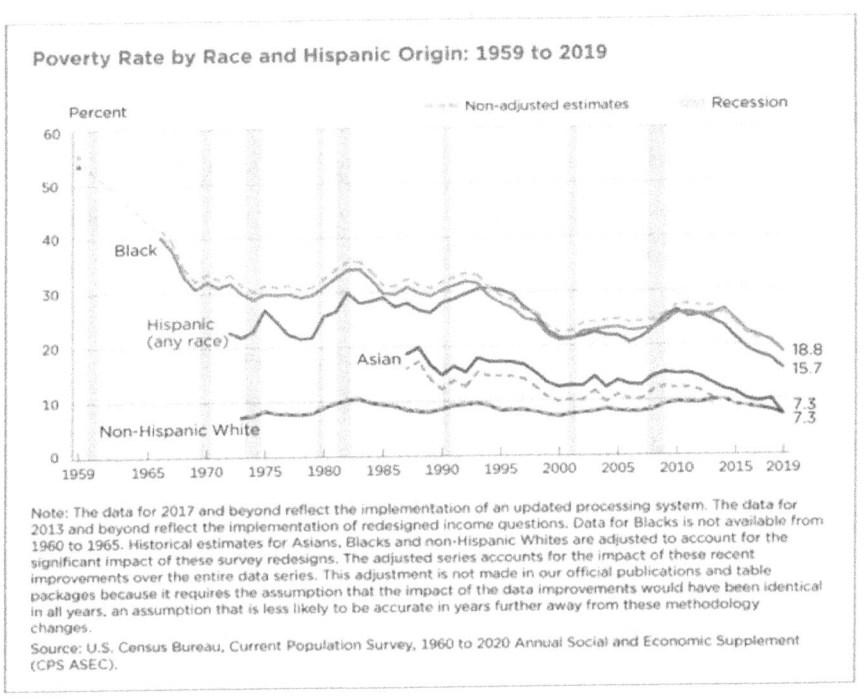

While the general trend indicates that poverty levels have declined for all races over time, the Non-Hispanic White line remains both steadier and lower. Despite current efforts to address racial inequality, poverty rates between races have a clear disparity. So why are low-income communities disproportionately POC?

Redlining

Although redlining now refers to all racial discrimination in housing, its origins lie in government maps. Officials would draw **red lines** around neighborhoods considered "risky investments," exclusively due to a high concentration of Black inhabitants.

This effectively blocked Black families' access to credit, insurance, and healthcare—most importantly, loans backed by government insurance programs. Further, these redlined communities lacked basic amenities like supermarkets and green spaces.—natural and recreational areas that are often lacking in neighborhoods subjected to this discriminatory practice, highlighting a form of environmental inequality.

By the time the Fair Housing Act was passed in 1968, which prohibited housing discrimination, properties that had previously been financially feasible had risen in value and were now unaffordable.[130]

The racial wealth gap is extremely important in predicting the future. However, it is larger than what we are often told. Statistically, Black families will earn less money than their white counterparts even after attending college. Additionally, POC-owned homes tend to sell for less on housing markets than white-owned ones do.

Over-Policing

Over-policing is defined as a tendency or policy "to police excessively, as by maintaining a large police presence or by responding aggressively to minor offenses."[131]

Most people have heard the myth that lower-income communities need more civil authority due to higher rates of crime. However, this is a paradox in itself.

---

130   Candace Jackson, "What Is Redlining?," The New York Times, August 17, 2021, https://www.nytimes.com/2021/08/17/realestate/what-is-redlining.html.

131   "Definition of Overpolice," in Www.Dictionary.Com, n.d., https://www.dictionary.com/browse/overpolice.

For example, take two identical communities with equal rates of crime. One location, however, has a police force of 10 while the other has 30. The community with 10 police officers will catch less crime, as they simply have fewer officers on duty. Thus, this skewed rate of "more crime" allows governments to incorrectly justify allocating more officers and perpetuate the cycle of over-policing.

Incarceration

There is plenty of evidence of racial bias in stop searches and arrests. An example of this is the investigation of the Ferguson Police Department,[132] for which the primary findings show racial bias.

Despite Black people making up 67% of the population in Ferguson between 2012 and 2014, they were subjected to:

- 85% of vehicle stops
- 90% of tickets
- 93% of arrests

Further, despite being 26% less likely to be in possession of illegal substances or weapons, Black people were more than twice as likely as white people[133] to be searched during traffic stops, even after adjusting for associated characteristics.

---

132 "Investigation of the Ferguson Police Department," justice.gov, March 4, 2015, https://www.justice.gov/sites/default/files/opa/press-releases/attachments/2015/03/04/ferguson_police_department_report.pdf.

133 Radley Balko, "There's Racial Bias in Our Police Systems. Here's the Overwhelming Proof.," Washington Post, June 11, 2020, https://www.washingtonpost.com/graphics/2020/opinions/systemic-racism-police-evidence-criminal-justice-system/.

A larger-scale investigation of racial inequities in police stops analyzed over 100 million traffic stops across America.[134] According to this examination, the threshold for examining the vehicles of Black and Hispanic drivers is considerably lower than the threshold for white drivers. Additionally, after sunset, when a "veil of darkness" covers one's race, Black drivers are less likely to be stopped.

There have also been studies depicting biases of judges, juries, prosecutors. According to an extensive multivariate regression study, federal sentences for Black male criminals are 19.1% greater[135] than for white male offenders in the same socioeconomic bracket.

Biased Incarceration

Biased incarceration is a stark manifestation of systemic racism, deeply ingrained in the fabric of the criminal justice system. Disproportionate arrest rates, sentencing practices, and incarceration levels for people of color, particularly Black and Hispanic communities, underscore a troubling reality.

This bias is not just a reflection of individual prejudices but is indicative of structural inequities that permeate law enforcement, judicial processes, and correctional systems. For instance, drug offenses are prosecuted more harshly when involving minorities, despite similar rates of drug use across racial and ethnic groups. The repercussions are profound, extending beyond the prison walls to

---

134   https://pubmed.ncbi.nlm.nih.gov/32367028/

135   "Demographic Differences in Sentencing: An Update to the 2012 Booker Report," ussc.gov, n.d., https://www.ussc.gov/sites/default/files/pdf/research-and-publications/research-publications/2017/20171114_Demographics.pdf.

affect families, communities, and perpetuating a cycle of disadvantage and marginalization.

The "School to Prison Pipeline" is a distressing pathway that highlights the intersection between education and the criminal justice system, further entrenching biased incarceration. This phenomenon describes how children, predominantly from minority and low-income backgrounds, are funneled out of public schools and into the juvenile and criminal justice systems.

Factors such as zero-tolerance policies, inadequate educational resources, and school-based arrests mean that minor infractions can lead to major consequences, disproportionately impacting students of color. The pipeline not only deprives children of their right to education but also exposes them to the criminal justice system at a young age, significantly increasing the likelihood of incarceration in their future and affecting their rights later on in life.

Something to keep in mind is that felons cannot vote. Thus, the higher rates of incarceration for Black men also deprives them of their political power to enact change within our system. Systemic racism continues to cast a long shadow over the United States, with the 2020 election cycle exposing deep-seated disparities affecting communities of color, particularly in poor Black counties.

For example, reports of voter suppression tactics, such as the disproportionate closure of polling places or the purging of voter rolls, predominantly impacted these communities, echoing the historical struggle for equal voting rights. Additionally, the pandemic's disproportionate impact on Black communities, coupled with economic disparities and healthcare access, highlighted and exacerbated existing racial inequities. The convergence of these factors in the 2020 election and beyond serves as a stark reminder of the pervasive nature of systemic racism and its profound implications on the democratic participation and overall well-being of Black communities in America.

Addressing this pipeline is crucial in dismantling systemic racism and reforming both the educational and criminal justice systems to create a more equitable society.

Media

Unfortunately, racial bias also holds influence in the news channels within the country. Without even realizing it, many of us have consumed a media narrative that depicts POC in a negative light.

For example,[136] look at how the Associated Press referred to 18-year-old Michael Brown who was a Black young adult. He was shot by a white police officer in Ferguson, Missouri in 2014, and was described as a "man." In addition to depriving Brown of his childhood, media also portrayed him as a "thug" and a criminal.

How has systemic racism played a part in your life?

(START: Trigger Warning: Police Brutality, Violence, Death)

---

136   Anastasia Tsioulcas, "Some Are Calling the Buffalo Suspect a 'teenager.' Is That a Privilege of His Race?," NPR.org, May 16, 2022, https://www.npr.org/2022/05/16/1099137936/some-are-calling-the-buffalo-suspect-a-teenager-is-that-a-privilege-of-his-race.

Section III: Systemic and Unjust Violence

Now that we understand a bit better how racial bias appears, we can delve further into it. It is more than an unjust disadvantage, it is dangerous and even fatal.

Dylann Roof, a white 21-year-old who had just killed nine Black churchgoers in Charleston, South Carolina, was given a Burger King lunch after he was apprehended. In 2020, white 17-year-old Kyle Rittenhouse shot two individuals in Kenosha, Wisconsin, killing them both. He was peacefully brought into custody by police and without injury.

Contrarily, even younger Black victims of police violence have been killed disproportionately, some of the most well-known being Tamir Rice and Eljah McClain.

A Case Study on Elijah McClain[137]

On August 24, 2019, just after 10:30 pm, the Aurora Police Department got a complaint regarding a "strange individual" flailing his hands and wearing an open face ski mask. This individual was later identified as McClain, who was listening to music and was often cold as he suffered from anemia.

Three police officers were sent to investigate. McClain, who was unarmed and not suspected of any crime, was, by police reports,

---

137   Lucy Tompkins, "Here's What You Need to Know About Elijah McClain's Death," The New York Times, January 19, 2022, https://www.nytimes.com/article/who-was-elijah-mcclain.html.

resisting arrest. Instead, The New York Times[138] reports that McClain "vomited several times, for which he apologized, saying 'I'm sorry, I wasn't trying to do that, I can't breathe correctly,'" while the officers put him in a now-illegal carotid hold, restricting his airways.

In the bodycam footage, Mr. McClain can be seen pleading with the cops to release their hold on him and moving aside.

Most notably, the police said that because all three of their cameras had fallen off after, that they had no evidence of their claim that McClain had tried to reach for one of their guns. Further, when questioned, they had contradicting stories of which officer's gun McClain had attempted to grab.

The police cited this as their justification for using force, as well as his "agitated mental state."[139] The term "excited delirium"[140] has become a catch-all for deaths that occur in the context of law enforcement restraint, often coinciding with substance use or mental illness, and disproportionately used to explain the deaths of young Black men in police encounters. This was also used in Derek Chauvin's defense in the George Floyd case.

---

138   Tompkins, "Here's What You Need to Know About Elijah McClain's Death," January 19, 2022.

139   Claire Lampen, "What We Know About the Killing of Elijah McClain," The Cut, September 1, 2021, https://www.thecut.com/2021/09/the-killing-of-elijah-mcclain-everything-we-know.html.

140   Julia Jones, "Authorities Claimed These Black Men Had Excited Delirium Just before They Died. But the Diagnosis Itself Is a Problem and Should Be Abandoned, a New Study Says," CNN, March 12, 2022, https://edition.cnn.com/2022/03/12/us/excited-delirium-police-deaths-study/index.html.

DEI and Anti-Racism Initiatives

When paramedics arrived, they injected McClain with a dosage of the medical sedative ketamine for a 200-pound person,[141] despite the fact that McClain weighed 140 pounds. Further, paramedics did not speak to, touch, or check his vital signs; he was already handcuffed when they administered the ketamine. He fell unconscious immediately.

McClain experienced a heart attack while traveling to the hospital. He was pronounced brain-dead; a few days later, he passed away. His relatives had said that he was covered in bruises.

The three police officers and two paramedics were charged with manslaughter and criminally negligent homicide two years after McClain's death.

The Biases That Contributed

1. Aging Children into Adults

    - As we previously discussed in the example of the Associated Press, media outlets have often portrayed Black boys, or even children, as men. Unfortunately, this is not an isolated incident; it is a reflection on the larger societal perception of Black children, including the hyper-sexualization of Black girls.

    - A study was conducted[142] to measure degrees of racial prejudice and impression of innocence involving both

---

141 Jennifer Kovaleski, "Aurora Paramedics Gave Maximum Dose of Ketamine Even When Patient's Weight Was Unknown," Denver 7 Colorado News, October 2, 2020, https://www.denver7.com/news/investigations/aurora-paramedics-gave-maximum-dose-of-ketamine-even-when-patients-weight-was-unknown.

142 "Black Boys Viewed as Older, Less Innocent Than Whites, Research Finds," apa.org, 2014, https://www.apa.org/news/press/releases/2014/03/black-boys-older.

students and police personnel. Within this, they found that Black boys are more likely to be viewed as criminals or unreliable from a young age (10 years old), and they are also more likely to experience police assault.

2. Exaggeration of Formidability and Physical Size
    - According to the findings of three[143] different studies on perception and racial bias, individuals tend to view Black males as being bigger and more dangerous than similarly sized white men.

Participants also agreed that police would be more justified in using force to restrain Black men even if they were unarmed because of an incorrect assumption that they were more likely to be able to cause harm in conflict. Elijah was 5'6 and 140 pounds.

(END: Trigger Warning, Police Brutality)

Case Study: Texturism in the Natural Hair Community

Texturism

Texturism[144] is the "discrimination faced by those with coarser and more Afro-textured hair. Texturism is based on the premise that

---

143 John Paul Wilson, Kurt Hugenberg, and Nicholas O. Rule, "Racial Bias in Judgments of Physical Size and Formidability: From Size to Threat.," Journal of Personality and Social Psychology 113, no. 1 (July 2017): 59–80, https://doi.org/10.1037/pspi0000092.

144 Janice Gassam Asare PhD, "4c Hair Discrimination: An Exploration Of Texturism," August 22, 2022, https://www.linkedin.com/pulse/4c-hair-discrimination-exploration-texturism-asare-ph-d-.

hair textures closer to white are more acceptable and is an extension of colorism, an issue plaguing the Black community for decades. Colorism[145] is "prejudice or discrimination against individuals with a dark skin tone, typically among people of the same ethnic or racial group."

In order to challenge this and embrace the natural beauty of Black features, the natural hair movement was created and has gained momentum over recent years. The natural hair movement—which was also prevalent in the 1960s and 70s—encourages men and women of African descent to embrace and celebrate our natural afro-textured hair, but it is evident that not all curl textures and types are appreciated within the community.[146] Even though the movement was created so that all afro-textured hair can be embraced and celebrated, light-skinned[147] women and girls with longer, looser curls have seemed to be the face and the beauty standard within the natural hair community, and they are often represented more when the discussion of natural hair comes about. On the other hand, it is evident that there is underrepresentation and curl discrimination toward Black women and girls with kinkier hair textures, such as with 4b and 4c hair facing negative stigma like being viewed as "nappy" and "undone." This all

---

145 "Colorism," in The Merriam-Webster.Com Dictionary, n.d., https://www.merriam-webster.com/dictionary/colorism.

146 Necessary Behavior, "The Natural Hair Movement: History, Stigma, and Successes," Necessary Behavior, May 5, 2021, https://www.necessarybehavior.com/blogs/news/the-natural-hair-movement-history-stigma-and-successes.

147 Zeba Blay, "Let's Talk About Colorism In The Natural Hair Community," HuffPost, January 8, 2016, https://www.huffpost.com/entry/lets-talk-about-colorism-in-the-natural-hair-community_n_566df1dfe4b011b83a6ba4f0.

leads back to the negative effects that colorism has had on the Black community.

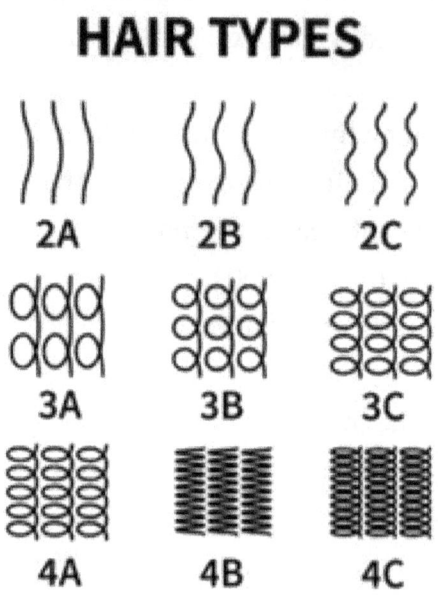

Texturism's Roots

The views on hair texture and the unappreciation of kinky and coily hair types all stem from the long history of colorism within the Black community. The issues of colorism amongst Black and Brown people came about because colorism[148] was often used by European colonists to create division between enslaved peoples and further the idea that being as close to white as possible was the ideal image. Unfortunately, this has had long-lasting effects on what is considered

---

[148] Mahima Rahman, "Digital Commons Wayne State," https://digitalcommons.wayne.edu/cgi/viewcontent.cgi?article=1069&context=honorstheses, December 14, 2020, https://digitalcommons.wayne.edu/cgi/viewcontent.cgi?article=1069.

"beautiful" within the Black community, and the beauty of darker features and kinkier hair is viewed as less than because those features do not closely mirror Eurocentric or white features.

Different laws and policies have only contributed to the negative stigma that comes with Black hair. A key example are laws prohibiting natural black hair and hairstyles frequently worn by members of the Black community from being worn in a school or workplace setting. Thankfully, efforts have been made to combat hair texture discrimination. One way this has been done is through a California proposed law called The CROWN Act,[149] which stands for "Creating a Respectful and Open World for Natural Hair," this law prohibits race-based hair discrimination, which is the denial of employment and educational opportunities because of hair texture or protective hairstyles. This groundbreaking law has only been enacted in 18 states,[150] and, unfortunately, race-based hair discrimination is still federally acceptable, meaning that young girls and women can still be written up or kicked out of school or their place of employment simply because of their hair texture or how they choose to style their hair.

Black children have historically faced discrimination by school officials and their peers for how they wear their hair. In 2018, an

---

[149] "H.R.2116 - Creating a Respectful and Open World for Natural Hair Act of 2022," Congress.gov, n.d., https://www.congress.gov/bill/117th-congress/house-bill/2116/text.

[150] Matt Gonzales, "CROWN Act: Does Your State Prohibit Hair Discrimination?," SHRM, August 19, 2022, https://www.shrm.org/resourcesandtools/hr-topics/behavioral-competencies/global-and-cultural-effectiveness/pages/crown-act-does-your-state-prohibit-hair-discrimination.aspx.

11-year-old girl in Louisiana[151] was asked to leave her class because school officials claimed that how she wore her braids violated school rules as she had "extensions." Following that same week, a six-year-old in Florida[152] was sent home on his first day of school because school administrators did not believe it was appropriate for him to wear his natural hair in locs. It is very sad to see, and it happens way too often that Black students are villainized and their education disrupted just because their natural hair and hairstyles are deemed inappropriate by school officials. Afro-textured hair[153] does not fit into the Eurocentric beauty standards that have been long accepted within this country, but we need to work towards changing the narrative because all hair is beautiful, from every loc to every kink and coil.

Combating the toxic views of texturism is not easy, but we can work towards changing the narrative to embracing and loving all hair types and textures. We can shift the narrative through visibility and representation in media and pop culture. Representing all hair types and features in the media matters because it influences the public mindset. Another way we can genuinely change is by starting from within and working towards shifting our mindset and perception around what beauty means. All natural hair is beautiful and unique, and we have to work towards creating an acceptable environment for all.

---

151   Julia Jacobs and Dan Levin, "Black Girl Sent Home From School Over Hair Extensions," The New York Times, August 22, 2018, https://www.nytimes.com/2018/08/21/us/black-student-extensions-louisiana.html.

152   Jacobs and Levin, "Black Girl Sent Home From School Over Hair Extensions."

153   "Black Women and Identity: What's Hair Got to Do With It?," n.d., https://quod.lib.umich.edu/cgi/t/text/text-idx?cc=mfsfront;c=mfs;c=mfsfront;idno=ark5583.0022.105;view=text;rgn=main;xc=1;g=mfsg.

Section IV: How do we Mitigate Racial and Social Injustice?

Well, we have to start at the core: systemic racism. Addressing racial bias and closing the racial wealth gap is a step towards a more equitable world.

Methods to Address Systemic Racism
- Education on systemic racism
- Increasing resources[154] such as educational opportunities, safe transportation, and teaching the power to self-advocate[155] for marginalized communities
- Advocate for, but never speaking over minority voices
- Supporting grassroots organizations[156] and providing funding
- Protections against unlawful restrictions on voting
- Enforcing fair housing policies

Methods to address Racial Violence
- Create innovative strategies for courts and community engagement
- Implement community-based safety models

---

154   "Gun Violence, Prevention of (Position Paper)," AAFP, n.d., https://www.aafp.org/about/policies/all/gun-violence.html.

155   "Address Gun Violence by Going After the Root Causes," Brennan Center for Justice, November 17, 2022, https://www.brennancenter.org/our-work/analysis-opinion/address-gun-violence-going-after-root-causes.

156   Shannon Frattaroli, "Grassroots Advocacy for Gun Violence Prevention: A Status Report on Mobilizing a Movement," Journal of Public Health Policy 24, no. 3/4 (2003): 332, https://doi.org/10.2307/3343381.

- Implement more social workers and mental health professionals in the response to 911 call. In New York, clinical social workers join police officers when responding to a 911 call
- Support neighborhood amenities[157] including housing, health care, and education, as well as more robust economic and employment prospects
  - Accepting such policies will reduce the need for enforcement, which in turn will reduce violent conflicts — especially in communities of color, those that are disadvantaged economically, and those who are overpoliced.
- Gun Policy Change[158]: Increase background checks, requirements for licensing,[159] and education about racial gun violence

We know, this is a heavy topic. Take a breather; you did great. Here are some positive news of the great work people are doing to save lives:

The CAHOOTS program in Eugene, Oregon, exemplifies an effective community-based safety model, where specialized teams adept in crisis

---

157   Colleen Walsh, "Solving Racial Disparities in Policing," Harvard Gazette, February 24, 2021, https://news.harvard.edu/gazette/story/2021/02/solving-racial-disparities-in-policing/.

158   Quoctrung Bui, Alicia Parlapiano, and Margot Sanger-Katz, "The Mass Shootings Where Stricter Gun Laws Might Have Made a Difference," The New York Times, June 5, 2022, https://www.nytimes.com/interactive/2022/06/04/upshot/mass-shooting-gun-laws.html.

159   "Policies That Reduce Gun Violence: Firearm Purchaser Licensing," Johns Hopkins Bloomberg School of Public Health, July 23, 2021, https://publichealth.jhu.edu/2021/policies-that-reduce-gun-violence-firearm-purchaser-licensing.

resolution, mental health, and emergency medicine, supplement police efforts. By redirecting appropriate 911 calls to these teams, the program demonstrates significant results: of the 25,000 calls received in 2017, only 250 needed police intervention. This approach, which involves unarmed specialists managing non-violent incidents including traffic stops, could significantly reduce violent police encounters.

Cheat Code Review

- Racism is a systemic, not a systematic, issue. This distinction recognizes that the issue resides within the larger systems within society rather than just individuals.
- Redlining, over-policing, and biased incarceration are all examples of systemic racism.
- Racial bias has negatively influenced the media and its coverage of racial injustices.
- Teaching self-advocacy, financially supporting grassroots organizations, promoting voter protections, and enforcing fair housing policies are methods to address systemic racism.

Chapter 8
DEI and Ethnic Studies

Written by: Kenny Lang, Kat Lin, Nyah Perez, & Brandon Choi

Section I: History of Ethnic Studies

Before we dive into the history of **ethnic studies**, it's important to first understand what they are. **Ethnic studies** is an umbrella term for the field of critical race studies that focuses on the experience of oppressed groups such as Black Americans, Indigenous People, Latines, and Asian Americans.

In the United States, the experiences of these oppressed groups are often connected to **white supremacy** and **systemic racism**.

- **White supremacy**: the belief that white people are a superior race and should dominate society, leading to the exclusion and oppression of other racial and ethnic groups.

- **Systemic racism**: a form of racism embedded in laws and regulations of a society that often discriminate ethnic and racial groups in areas like housing, healthcare, employment, education and politics.

The purpose of ethnic studies is to develop fundamental skills in critical and global thinking and comparative analysis, as well as an understanding of the interactions of race, class, gender, and sexuality in the experiences of a range of social groups.

The history of ethnic studies started in California in the late 1960s from the **Third World Liberation Front** at San Francisco State University. The Third World Liberation Front was a coalition of the Black Student Union, Latin American Students Organization, Filipino American Students Organization, the Asian American Political Alliance, and Mexican American student Organization. These coalitions worked together to challenge the oppressive structures of universities and ensure the stories of marginalized ethnic communities were heard. Their original demands included:

1. Increased access to higher education for students of color[160]
2. Increased hiring of faculty of color[161]
3. A Third World College[162] dedicated to the often-ignored histories of oppressed ethnic groups such as Asian Americans, African Americans, Native Americans and Latines

The strikes of the Third World Liberation Front were the longest student strikes in history. The protests lasted three months long but did not result in the development of a Third World College. Instead, the first departments of ethnic studies at San Francisco State University and University of California Berkeley were created.

---

160   Amanda Morrison PhD, "What Is Ethnic Studies?," https://academicsenate.santarosa.edu/, n.d., https://academicsenate.santarosa.edu/sites/academicsenate.santarosa.edu/files/documents/A_Morrison_OPEN_FORUM_What+Is+Ethnic+Studies_07_22_2020.pdf.

161   Morrison, "What Is Ethnic Studies?"

162   Morrison, "What Is Ethnic Studies?"

Case Study

Student Organizing: Diversify Our Narrative

Today, many student activists continue the legacy of the Third World Liberation by fighting for more racially diverse educational materials in classrooms. However, current students have taken their activism online and are using social media as a means of resistance. Social media has often been criticized in activist spaces because it has been used for performative activism. However, when used towards the right causes, social media can be a beneficial tool. One prime example of this is the online petition turned full-blown campaign known as Diversify Our Narrative (DON).[163]

Diversify Our Narrative is a grassroots organization founded in 2020 by Stanford students Jasmine Nguyen (left) and Katelin Zhou (right). Nguyen and Zhou saw the lack of racially diverse texts in public schools as a key issue in how students understood race and racism. As a result, the pair decided to create a petition, which called for more books by BIPOC (Black, Indigenous, and People of Color) authors in English classes. Nguyen and Zhou utilized the hashtag #DiversifyOurNarrative on social media as a way to spread awareness about their campaign.

Jasmine Nguyen and Katelin Zhou's initial campaign evolved into an entire organization. DON now provides multidisciplinary lesson plans where they cite critical BIPOC scholars such as Cathy

---

163 "Diversify Our Narrative," https://www.diversifyournarrative.com/, n.d., https://www.diversifyournarrative.com/.

Park Hong, Ta-Nehisi Coates, and many others.[164] Additionally, the organization encourages students to get involved, not just on social media but in their own schools. They currently have regional chapters across the country[165] and have resources for students interested in implementing DON lesson plans or materials in their classrooms.

Diversify Our Narrative continues to utilize social media as a channel for activism. Students, teachers, and parents can digitally engage with their project via the infographics they post, mainly, on their Instagram.[166] Infographics are social media posts that contain information about social movements in a way that is brief and easy to understand. Although these posts cannot cover the entirety of an issue, they serve as helpful starting points for anyone to learn about a particular topic!

---

164 "Lesson Plans," Diversity Our Narrative, n.d., https://www.diversifyournarrative.com/lesson-plans?

165 "Our Chapters," Diversity Our Narrative, n.d., https://www.diversifyournarrative.com/our-chapters.

166 "@DiversifyOurNarrative," Instagram, n.d., http://www.instagram.com/diversifyournarrative.

Infographic from DON's Instagram

While DON is a standout voice in the push towards education curriculum reform, there are thousands of other organizations who advocate for racially diverse teaching(s) and ethnic studies.[167] Being a part of local movements is extremely important and easy to do. Many of these community-based organizations were created on the simple fact that these individuals saw a need for a more diverse curriculum and understood the fundamentals of social media publicity. As a result, any student can truly get involved and make a difference in their community, so long as they take the first steps to do so.

Section II: Current views on Ethnic Studies

Currently, ethnic studies has been a hot and controversial topic of conversation, especially within US high schools and universities. There's also a stark difference in the inclusion of ethnic studies in the curriculum of West Coast and East Coast schools. There has not been research on why the East Coast has significantly fewer ethnic study programs, but it is clear that there have been no significant, widespread demands in the East Coast for the inclusion of ethnic studies in K-12 schools. However, there have been smaller coalitions such as the development of Asian American Studies Departments at University of Massachusetts, Boston and Hunter College in New York.

---

167 Terry Nguyen, "Student Activists Want Their Schools to Adopt an Anti-Racist Education," Vox, July 29, 2020, https://www.vox.com/identities/2020/7/29/21345114/students-diversify-curriculum-change-antiracist.

Outside of the marginalized communities already mentioned, can you think of other communities you'd want to see ethnic studies on?

The argument against ethnic studies stems from a belief they can be potentially harmful and promote resentment towards a specific race or class of people.[168] Additional arguments claim that it can increase racial tensions and radicalize students, but this is a short-sighted myth. Ethnic studies focus on teaching students the historic backgrounds of oppressed communities, rather than inflammatory claims about race and ethnic relations.

The controversy surrounding ethnic studies also stems from the ban on the Mexican American ethnic studies program in Arizona. In Tucson, Arizona, Mexican American students who took Mexican American Studies classes were more likely[169] to graduate from high school and even to pass standardized tests they had previously failed. Despite these positive outcomes, Tucson's Mexican American Studies program was wrongfully terminated through the passage of a state law that banned all such programs.

Case Study

Arizona's Ban on Ethnic Studies

---

168   Julie Depenbrock, "Ethnic Studies: A Movement Born Of A Ban," NPR.org, August 13, 2017, https://www.npr.org/sections/ed/2017/08/13/541814668/ethnic-studies-a-movement-born-of-a-ban.

169   Holly Yettick, "Academic Benefits of Mexican-American Studies Reaffirmed in New Analysis," Education Week, October 5, 2022, https://www.edweek.org/teaching-learning/academic-benefits-of-mexican-american-studies-reaffirmed-in-new-analysis/2014/11.

In 2010, Republican lawmakers, Tom Horne and John Huppenthal, passed HB 2281, which prohibited classes and materials that promoted "ethnic solidarity,"[170] or "resentment toward a race or class or people." The Mexican American ethnic studies program at Tucson High School was affected, as Horne and Huppenthal claimed the program was increasing racial tensions. In their arguments, they cited the use of Freire's Pedagogy of the Oppressed and Rodolfo Acuña's Occupied America in the program's materials, in an attempt to support the argument that ethnic studies promotes revolution and the government being overthrown.

Horne and Huppenthal's arguments wrongfully targeted the Mexican American studies program at Tucson High School, where 88% of the students are minorities. African American studies were not negatively affected by the passing of this bill, revealing the prejudiced and inconsistent undertones of the bill.

In August 2017, federal judge Wallace Tashima cited HB 2281 as a violation of students' rights and lifted the ban on ethnic studies that was in place for seven years. In his ruling, Judge Tashima stated, "Both enactment and enforcement were motivated by racial animus,"[171] as the Mexican American studies program was the only ethnic studies named in the bill.

While the ban on ethnic studies in Arizona being struck down was a win for ethnic studies across the country, it is still unknown whether

---

170   Depenbrock, "Ethnic Studies: A Movement Born Of A Ban," August 13, 2017.
171   Julie Depenbrock and Julie Depenbrock, "Federal Judge Finds Racism Behind Arizona Law Banning Ethnic Studies," NPR.org, August 23, 2017, https://www.npr.org/sections/ed/2017/08/22/545402866/federal-judge-finds-racism-behind-arizona-law-banning-ethnic-studies.

or not the Mexican American studies program at Tucson High School was restored.

Section III: Why should we care?

Now that you've learned what ethnic studies is and the controversy behind it, it's time to understand why it's important and what we can do to continue the inclusion of ethnic studies in our schools and universities. Let's take a look at the impacts of ethnic studies on students!

- The National Education Association[172] found when students of different ages take ethnic studies, they consistently experience "academic achievement, high level of awareness of race and racism, and positive identification with one's own racial group."
- An additional study[173] done in 2016 by the Stanford Graduate School of Education also found that a "high school ethnic studies course [...] boosted attendance and academic performance of students at risk of dropping out," Stanford News reports.
- Teachers of ethnic studies also argue[174] that these courses help students break cycles of trauma, violence, and poverty that ethnic and marginalized communities often face.

---

172   "The Fight for Ethnic Studies," Learning for Justice, n.d., https://www.learningforjustice.org/magazine/spring-2021/the-fight-for-ethnic-studies.
173   Christine Sleeter and Miguel Zavala, "WHAT THE RESEARCH SAYS ABOUT ETHNIC STUDIES," National Education Association, n.d., https://www.nea.org/sites/default/files/2020-10/What%20the%20Research%20Says%20About%20Ethnic%20Studies.
174   Depenbrock, Julie. "Ethnic Studies: A Movement Born Of A Ban." NPR.org, August 13, 2017.

Ethnic studies provide[175] a critical lens for students, especially POC, to examine and contextualize the injustices currently happening to marginalized communities. It's about active resistance, listening, engaging, and can even be healing. These courses provide students with the ability to connect their experiences to larger events and issues. When students can connect their experiences to a larger context, a positive transformation can occur. Ethnic studies allow unheard stories to be told and can help students feel seen and heard. Reaffirming students' experiences are valid, especially in the classroom, is a transformative experience and can go on to shape student's lives and academic careers.

Case Study

BTS and the AAPI Movement

Anti-Asian Hate Crimes

From the beginning of the COVID-19 pandemic until now, there has been a rising trend of Asian American hate crimes. According to data[176] from March of 2021, one in six Asian Americans expressed that they had experienced a hate crime, and, more recently at the beginning of 2022, that figure was one in twelve. However, this

---

175 Sleeter and Zavala, "WHAT THE RESEARCH SAYS ABOUT ETHNIC STUDIES."

176 Frances Kai-Hwa Wang, "How Violence against Asian Americans Has Grown and How to Stop It, According to Activists," PBS NewsHour, April 11, 2022, https://www.pbs.org/newshour/nation/a-year-after-atlanta-and-indianapolis-shootings-targeting-asian-americans-activists-say-we-cant-lose-momentum.

surge in racism towards Asian Americans is not a new topic, as in the past years similar events occurred where specific minority groups were targeted due to the current events. Recent data[177] reveals that the percentage of Americans who believed Asian Americans had some fault in spreading the virus jumped from 10% to 20% between 2021 and 2022, which partially explains why Asian Americans have been the recent targets of hate crimes. There was an increase in the percentage of Americans who felt it was appropriate to call the virus the "Wuhan Virus" or "Chinese Virus" from 11% in 2021 to 21% in 2022.

One such example of a crime[178] that targeted Asian Americans occurred on March 16th, where six Asian women were killed in an Atlanta spa shooting.

Voice Amidst Violence

Bangtan Sonyeondan,[179] or otherwise known as BTS, is a world-renowned K-pop (Korean pop) group that has left a lasting impression on many people through the messages that they have spread through their music. As an international group, they have been able to produce several US billboard hits and generated more interest in Korean

---

177   Jennifer Lee, "Confronting the Invisibility of Anti-Asian Racism," Brookings, May 18, 2022, https://www.brookings.edu/blog/how-we-rise/2022/05/18/confronting-the-invisibility-of-anti-asian-racism/.

178   "More Than 9,000 Anti-Asian Incidents Have Been Reported Since The Pandemic Began," NPR.org, August 13, 2021, https://www.npr.org/2021/08/12/1027236499/anti-asian-hate-crimes-assaults-pandemic-incidents-aapi.

179   "PROFILE | BTS | BIGHIT MUSIC," n.d., https://ibighit.com/bts/eng/profile/.

culture in the process. One such example[180] is with Mr. Hernandez, a teacher from Los Angeles, California, who was inspired by BTS's popularity to create one of the first Korean American Culture and Society courses in the country.

BTS have also used their platforms as musicians to sing about topics such as self-love and racism. In their song "Change" by RM featuring Wale, the duo share their insights on racism and encourage their listeners to vote. BTS members have further utilized their platform through various channels, such as a speech[181] they gave at the United Nation. As representatives of Unicef, they discussed the importance of nurturing self-love within the youth and protecting children from violence.

BTS at The White House

In May of 2022, BTS was given the opportunity to speak at the White House with President Biden to discuss the recent surge in Anti-Asian hate crime. During the pre-meeting conference, member Suga voiced, "It's not wrong to be different. Equality begins when we open up and embrace all of our differences," addressing the importance of cultural acceptance and appreciation.[182] In their conversation with

---

180   "Here's How Boy Band BTS Inspired a School in South L.A. to Teach Korean Culture," Orange County Register, October 14, 2019, https://www.ocregister.com/2019/10/14/heres-how-boy-band-bts-inspired-a-school-in-south-l-a-to-teach-korean-culture/.
181   ""We Have Learned to Love Ourselves, so Now I Urge You to 'Speak Yourself.'"" n.d., https://www.unicef.org/press-releases/we-have-learned-love-ourselves-so-now-i-urge-you-speak-yourself.
182   Elizabeth Blair, "K-Pop Stars BTS Went to the White House to Talk about Anti-Asian Hate Crimes," NPR.org, June 1, 2022, https://www.npr.

President Biden, the group acknowledged the importance of wielding the platform given to them by their fans in a way that stands against the surge in violence against Asian Americans and other minority groups.[183] Following the aforementioned Atlanta spa shooting, BTS published a tweet. speaking out against the hate crime and in support of the StopAAPI Hate movement on their Twitter account of over 48 million followers.[184] BTS and their fan base have also been very active and vocal in the BLM movement as well as others.

Question:

Despite the overwhelming support that BTS has received for speaking about AAPI, there has also been criticism[185] that questions the appropriateness of them speaking for AAPIs, as they have not had the unique experience of being Asian in America. Despite this gap, how has their work contributed to the discussion surrounding diversity and ethnic studies?

What can we do? Where should we go next and why?

Supporting ethnic studies starts with honoring and respecting these respective departments within universities and K-12 schools. It starts with adequately funding these programs and staffing them

---

org/2022/05/31/1102244756/k-pop-stars-bts-went-to-the-white-house-to-talk-about-anti-asian-hate-crimes.

183   The White House, "President Biden and Vice President Harris Welcome BTS to the White House," YouTube, June 4, 2022, https://www.youtube.com/watch?v=fHFgJux7MzM.

184   " 방탄소년단 On," Twitter, March 30, 2021, https://twitter.com/BTS_twt/status/1376712834269159425?s=20.

185   Lenika Cruz, "When BTS Came to the White House," The Atlantic, June 8, 2022, https://www.theatlantic.com/culture/archive/2022/06/bts-white-house-visit-aapi-inclusion/661206/?utm_source=copy-link.

as well. Honor and respect the ethnic studies disciplines by focusing on African American and Africana/Black Studies, Indigenous People Studies, Asian American Studies, and Latino/Hispanic American Studies.

The fight for Ethnic Studies means working with other communities and groups and understanding the importance of activism and protest. To understand how to continue supporting ethnic studies, we need to look at how it was pioneered and rallied by the Third World Liberation Front.

Why should curriculum engage in equity work and culturally responsive content and practices?

Culturally responsive content is defined as information and practices that appreciate diversity and the importance of students' cultural references in learning. It is a philosophy of teaching and learning that attempts to equip both teachers and students with cultural nuances.

Curriculums should engage in equity work[186] to ensure students of all backgrounds feel seen and heard within history. This helps students feel empowered and connected to one another in class, even if they come from a diverse range of backgrounds.

An inclusive classroom and curriculum can also help students understand different perspectives and build empathy with people of all backgrounds. Engaging in equity work also requires community building and engagement, allowing students to further develop

---

186   "The Value of Creating a Culturally Responsive Curriculum for Diverse Student Populations," William Woods University, July 15, 2021, https://education-blog.williamwoods.edu/2021/07/creating-culturally-responsive-curriculum-for-diverse-student-population/.

better relationships and understanding of different backgrounds and communities of color.

Additionally, culturally responsive teaching methods[187] also help educators reflect on how their own identity and experiences affect their attitudes and teaching practices. Creating a culturally responsive classroom and curriculum can not only transform the student but also the teacher. This can lead to the next generation of culturally responsive educators who can create a more diverse, equitable, and inclusive environment for all students!

Ethnic studies is rooted in civic engagement and service, community collaboration. It's about being with communities and groups of all backgrounds and understanding them. While ethnic studies is crucial for people of color to understand their histories, cultures, and backgrounds, it's also important for all people to know the stories of historically oppressed communities and what can be done to empower them in the present. More so than the quizzes and exams, the benchmark goals of ethnic studies are community engagement and historically diverse curricula.

The fight for ethnic studies has come an incredibly long way, but it's far from over. While it is slowly being implemented in universities along the West and East Coasts, there is still a need for its recognition in K-12 schools, as well as globally.

What does ethnic studies mean to you? How can you advocate to implement the courses in your school?

---

187   "The Value of Creating a Culturally Responsive Curriculum for Diverse Student Populations."

DEI AND ETHNIC STUDIES

Cheat Code Recap

- Ethnic studies aim to focus on the experience of oppressed groups through the lens of critical race theory.
- There is a long history of controversy surrounding ethnic studies. Despite the criticism of its potentially inflammatory and divisive effects, ethnic studies have yielded positive results in academic performance and identity empowerment.

The Let's Talk About Diversity Cheat Code

CHAPTER 1: ABCs of DEI
- DEI stands for Diversity, Equity, and Inclusion.
- Diversity: a principle that promotes a variety of identities within a group of people, such as race, ethnicity, sexual orientation, gender, religious background, socioeconomic status, disability status, etc.
- Equity: a principle that promotes justice, impartiality, and fairness within the procedures, processes, and distributions of resources in institutions or systems.
- Inclusion: a principle that welcomes and supports individuals from diverse backgrounds
- Equality and Equity are two terms that have very different implications when discussing DEI!

CHAPTER 2: DEI in Educational Institutions
- Educational inequality ultimately leads to social inequality because education is one of the biggest vehicles of upward social mobility.
- Not all public schools provide the same quality of education; the ones in wealthier neighborhoods receive more funding that

enables them to provide better resources and more experienced instructors.
- Education has been historically used as a tool for oppression against marginalized populations, like Black Americans in the Jim Crow South.
- The education system has been exploited by wealthy individuals to gain an unfair advantage in college admissions; Operation Varsity Blues highlights this injustice.
- Affirmative action is an equitable form of college admissions that allows universities to take social factors such as race and class into consideration.

CHAPTER 3: DEI in the Workplace
- Diversity within the workplace promotes productivity.
- Microaggressions, discrimination, implicit biases, and harassment are all factors that harm DEI within the workplace.
- Diversity can be increased through hiring practices such as having a diverse hiring team, using diversity targets, and standardizing scoring to reduce biases.
- Harassment and microaggressions can be limited through reactionary actions and/or institutional change.

CHAPTER 4: DEI in Social Media & Branding
- Social media is a powerful tool and should be used responsibly by learning media literacy and practicing netiquette.
- Social media has served as a platform to catalyze and jumpstart social movements.

- Crowdfunding can be a great channel for individuals and organizations to receive financial support from people inside and outside of their direct communities.
- While social media has been used for positive social change, it is important to be mindful of performative activism and its harmful effects.
- Social media can be used to develop a brand's identity and communicate its story.

CHAPTER 5: DEI in Action
- DEI strategies are plans aimed to guide businesses and organizations in promoting DEI principles so that they can be more welcoming to all individuals.

CHAPTER 6: DEI in STEM
- The STEM fields are playing crucial roles in shaping current and future societies, so it is important that they are composed of diverse individuals.
- Minority representation in STEM is slow to increase, but numerous individuals and organizations are stepping up to increase awareness and provide opportunities.
- Methods to promoting diversity within STEM include establishing diversity offices, increasing course offerings in diverse schools, increasing financial aid opportunities, reforming college recruitment, and increasing awareness of existing opportunities.

CHAPTER 7: DEI and Anti-Racism Initiatives
- Racism is a systemic, not a systematic, issue. This distinction recognizes that the issue resides within the larger systems within society rather than just individuals.
- Redlining, over-policing, and biased incarceration are all examples of systemic racism.
- Racial bias has negatively influenced the media and its coverage of racial injustices.
- Teaching self-advocacy, financially supporting grassroots organizations, promoting voter protections, and enforcing fair housing policies are methods to address systemic racism.

CHAPTER 8: DEI & Ethnic Studies
- Ethnic studies aim to focus on the experience of oppressed groups through the lens of critical race theory.
- There is a long history of controversy surrounding ethnic studies. Despite the criticism of its potentially inflammatory and divisive effects, ethnic studies have yielded positive results in academic performance and identity empowerment.

Conclusion

Written by: Tiffany Yau & Brandon Choi

As we close this comprehensive exploration on Diversity, Equity, and Inclusion (DEI), it is evident that DEI is not merely a set of initials, but a crucial framework permeating every sector of our society. From the foundational ABCs of DEI that laid the groundwork for our understanding, to its significant role in educational institutions, the importance of fostering inclusivity and diversity cannot be overstated. The workplace, a cornerstone of adult life, has its unique set of challenges and opportunities in implementing DEI, as does the rapidly evolving realm of social media and branding.

By observing DEI in action, we witness its transformative power and the positive change it can bring. This is especially critical in fields like STEM, where historically, diverse voices have been underrepresented. With the rise of anti-racism initiatives and the push for ethnic studies, it's evident that DEI is more than just a trend—it's an essential part of a just and equitable future. As readers, it's our responsibility to take the insights and lessons from this book and apply them in our respective spheres, ensuring that DEI principles are more than words, but a lived reality for all.

For additional resources and online worksheets, visit: https://fulphil.org/class-projects

Glossary

CHAPTER 1: ABCs of DEI

Diversity: a principle that promotes a variety of identities within a group of people, such as race, ethnicity, sexual orientation, gender, religious background, socioeconomic status, disability status

Equity: a principle that promotes justice, impartiality, and fairness within the procedures, processes, and distributions of resources in institutions or systems

Inclusion: a principle that welcomes and supports individuals from diverse backgrounds

Equality: the state of providing the same opportunities and resources to all people

CHAPTER 2: ABCs and Educational Institutions

Ableism: bias against, or other harm directed towards people with disabilities

Blackfishing: the act of cultural appropriation that involves altering one's appearance to appear Black through makeup, digital editing, and other means.

Socioeconomic mobility: the ability of a person or group of people to rise up in socioeconomic class, often influenced by factors such as gender, race, ethnicity, age, education level, and current socioeconomic class.

Environmental racism: the trend where low income areas with higher populations of people of color tend to suffer from higher rates of pollution

Segregation: the historical act of separating people on the basis of race and/or gender, was a crucial component in the fight by Black Americans against the Jim Crow South.

Busing programs: programs that transported Black students to formerly all-white schools during the attempts at integration in the late 1950s South

Integration: attempts by the US government to have schools that allowed both Black and White students to attend, was mandated following the Supreme Court decision in Brown v. Board of Education (1954), was difficult to uphold and was implemented only in a few areas

Glossary

Minority advantage: the myth that providing marginalized communities with support and services is an act of discrimination against other groups and is putting them at a disadvantage

Affirmative action: policies that allow colleges/universities/workplaces/programs to equitably consider race, class, and demographic in their decisions

FGLI: acronym for first-generation and/or low income, usually a descriptor for university students

Common Core Standard: a country-wide standardized curriculum that implements shared benchmarks for progress, intended to set a higher standard for education quality through standards of accountability, lacking in its ability to consider the nuances of individual learning styles

CHAPTER 3: DEI in the Workplace

Affinity bias: human tendency to gravitate towards people similar to oneself

Microaggression: subtle remarks that communicate negative messages to an individual or group based on their minority identity

Implicit Bias: subconscious biases that are shaped by stereotypes perpetuated by society, can involuntarily and unintentionally shape one's thoughts, actions, and decisions

Harassment: unwelcome conduct and/or intimidation based on factors such as race, color, religion, gender, sexual orientation, national origin

Mental Health: an individual's psychological, emotional, and social well-being, influences one's thoughts, feelings, actions, responses to stress, and ability to connect with others

Tokenism: the act of including members from underrepresented groups in an exploitative effort to present the appearance of diversity rather than making a genuine effort to increase diversity

Reactionary action: an in-the-moment response to acts of bias, harassment, and microaggressions, a method to limit negative actions in the workplace and other organizations

Institutional change: change within the workplace aimed to prohibit harassment of any kind

CHAPTER 4: DEI in Social Media & Branding

Media literacy: the skill that helps people evaluate forms of media and understand the perspective they are being written from

Glossary

Algorithm: a computer process often implemented by social media companies to increase the engagement of users through prompting more engagement

Netiquette: the skill in carefully, mindfully, and intentionally interacting with social media and other online platforms

Infographics: images that contain condensed and relevant information on a key topic or issue, often used as a means of educating users on social media platforms

CHAPTER 5: DEI in Action

Crowdfunding: a form of raising financial resources for a cause by allowing individuals across the globe to donate

Performative activism: participating in activism for the sake of increasing one's own social capital rather than genuinely supporting the cause, also known as slacktivism

Brand development: the strategic process of creating a company's distinct image, involves the company's values, products, services, and how they promote these components

Texturism: discrimination faced by those with coarser and more Afro-textured hair, an extension of colorism

Colorism: prejudice or discrimination against individuals with a dark skin tone

CHAPTER 7: DEI and Anti-Racism Initiatives

Systematic: being consistently repeated

Systemic: being part of an entire system

Redlining: all forms of racial discrimination in housing, originated from government officials drawing red lines around "risky" neighborhoods with high concentrations of Black inhabitants, reduced access to credit, insurance, healthcare, and loans

Over-policing: the excessive policing done through the maintenance of a large police presence or aggressive responses to minor offenses, often occurring within communities with larger minority populations, feeds into the misconception that lower-income minority communities create higher rates of crime

CHAPTER 8: DEI & Ethnic Studies

Ethnic studies: an umbrella term for the field of critical race studies that encompasses the experiences of oppressed groups such as Black Americans, Indigenous People, Latines, and Asian Americans

White supremacy: the belief that white people are the superior race and should dominate society, leadings to the exclusion and oppression of other racial and ethnic groups

Third World Liberation Front: a coalition of the Black Student Union, the Latin American Students Organization, the Filipino American Students Organization, the Asian American Political Alliance and a Mexican American student Organization at San Francisco State University in the late 1960s , the original source of Ethnic Studies

Bibliography

1. "Defining DEI | Diversity, Equity & Inclusion | University of Michigan," n.d. https://diversity.umich.edu/about/defining-dei/.
2. Waterford.org. "Why Understanding Equity vs. Equality in Schools Can Help You Create an Inclusive Classroom," October 8, 2021. https://www.waterford.org/education/equity-vs-equality-in-education/.
3. "Diversity, Equity, and Inclusion – A Professional Development Offering of the Extension Foundation Impact Collaborative," n.d. https://dei.extension.org/.
4. "Diversity, Equity, and Inclusion – A Professional Development Offering of the Extension Foundation Impact Collaborative."
5. Center for Teaching Excellence. "Blog: 5 January 2020," January 5, 2020. https://cte.virginia.edu/blog/2020/01/05/diversity-and-inclusive-teaching-practices-stem.
6. "Blog: 5 January 2020."
7. Vaughn, Billy E. "THE HISTORY OF DIVERSITY TRAINING & ITS PIONEERS." Diversity Officer Magazine, June 17, 2018. https://diversityofficermagazine.com/diversity-inclusion/the-history-of-diversity-training-its-pioneers/
8. "THE HISTORY OF DIVERSITY TRAINING & ITS PIONEERS," June 17, 2018.

9. "THE HISTORY OF DIVERSITY TRAINING & ITS PIONEERS," June 17, 2018.
10. Juda, Edyta. "Equity vs. Equality: What's the Difference? | Online Public Health." GW-UMT, November 30, 2022. https://onlinepublichealth.gwu.edu/resources/equity-vs-equality/.
11. Kittner, Paul. "The Problem with That Equity vs. Equality Graphic You're Using." Cultural Organizing, October 30, 2016. https://culturalorganizing.org/the-problem-with-that-equity-vs-equality-graphic/.
12. Paul Kittner , Equality vs. Equity , October 30, 2016, Cultural Organizing , October 30, 2016, https://culturalorganizing.org/the-problem-with-that-equity-vs-equality-graphic/#.
13. Kittner, "The Problem with That Equity vs. Equality Graphic You're Using."
14. Kittner, "The Problem with That Equity vs. Equality Graphic You're Using."
15. "Why Understanding Equity vs. Equality in Schools Can Help You Create an Inclusive Classroom."
16. "Department of Education Equity Action Plan | US Department of Education," n.d. https://www.ed.gov/equity.
17. "Department of Education Equity Action Plan | US Department of Education.
18. Entrepreneur India. "Study Shows Public School Students Do Better Than Private School Students in College Admission to Top US Universities," August 18, 2020. https://www.entrepreneur.com/en-in/news-and-trends/study-shows-public-school-students-do-better-than-private/354897.

19. Murphy, James. "The Real College Admissions Scandal." Slate Magazine, June 14, 2021. https://slate.com/news-and-politics/2021/06/private-schools-competitive-college-advantage-problems.html.
20. Young, Robin, and Robert Pianta. "Family Income Affects Kids' Success More Than Public Vs. Private School, Study Finds | Here & Now." WBUR.org, August 27, 2018. https://www.wbur.org/hereandnow/2018/08/27/public-private-school-family-income-study.
21. Chen, Grace. "An Overview of the Funding of Public Schools." Public School Review, June 22, 2022. https://www.publicschoolreview.com/blog/an-overview-of-the-funding-of-public-schools.
22. "2.2 Poverty and Race: How Do Students' Backgrounds Affect Their School Performance? | ED100," n.d. https://ed100.org/lessons/poverty.
23. "Economic Impacts of Dropouts – National Dropout Prevention Center," n.d. https://dropoutprevention.org/resources/statistics/quick-facts/economic-impacts-of-dropouts/.
24. nces.ed.gov. "Immediate College Enrollment Rate," 2018. https://nces.ed.gov/programs/coe/pdf/Indicator_CPA/coe_cpa_2018_05.pdf.
25. Sasser, Nesa. "How Schools Motivate Students for State Testing." The Classroom | Empowering Students in Their College Journey, November 5, 2021. https://www.theclassroom.com/schools-motivate-students-state-testing-13290.html.

26. American Federation of Teachers. "Jim Crow's Schools," August 8, 2014. https://www.aft.org/periodical/american-educator/summer-2004/jim-crows-schools.
27. Browne-Marshall, Gloria. "Busing Ended 20 Years Ago. Today Our Schools Are Segregated Once Again." Time, September 11, 2019. https://time.com/5673555/busing-school-segregation/.
28. Pember, Mary Annette. "The Traumatic Legacy of Indian Boarding Schools." The Atlantic, January 6, 2022. https://www.theatlantic.com/education/archive/2019/03/traumatic-legacy-indian-boarding-schools/584293/.
29. McGregor, By Kameron Virk And Nesta. "Blackfishing: The Women Accused of Pretending to Be Black." BBC News, December 5, 2018. https://www.bbc.com/news/newsbeat-46427180.
30. Goldman, Tom. "A New Era Dawns In College Sports, As The NCAA Scrambles To Keep Up." NPR.org, June 28, 2021. https://www.npr.org/2021/06/28/1010129443/a-new-era-dawns-in-college-sports-as-the-ncaa-scrambles-to-keep-up.
31. Solomon, Jon. "Survey: African-American Youth More Often Play Sports to Chase College, pro Dreams." The Aspen Institute Project Play, October 26, 2022. https://www.aspenprojectplay.org/national-youth-sport-survey/african-american-youth-more-often-play-sports-to-chase-college-pro-dreams.
32. Dixon-RomÁN, Ezekiel J., Howard T. Everson, and John J. Mcardle. "Race, Poverty and SAT Scores: Modeling the Influences of Family Income on Black and White High School Students' SAT Performance." Teachers College Record: The

Voice of Scholarship in Education 115, no. 4 (April 2013): 1–33. https://doi.org/10.1177/016146811311500406.
33. Greenstone, Michael Adam Looney. "Education Is the Key to Better Jobs." Brookings, July 29, 2016. https://www.brookings.edu/blog/up-front/2012/09/17/education-is-the-key-to-better-jobs/.
34. "Evidence Matters: Understanding Neighborhood Effects of Concentrated Poverty | HUD USER," n.d. https://www.huduser.gov/portal/periodicals/em/winter11/highlight2.html.
35. Zajacova, Anna, and Elizabeth M. Lawrence. "The Relationship Between Education and Health: Reducing Disparities Through a Contextual Approach." Annual Review of Public Health 39, no. 1 (April 1, 2018): 273–89. https://doi.org/10.1146/annurev-publhealth-031816-044628.
36. Greenstone, "Education Is the Key to Better Jobs," July 29, 2016.
37. cdc.gov. "Health Insurance and Access to Care," February 2017. https://www.cdc.gov/nchs/data/factsheets/factsheet_hiac.pdf.
38. "Environmental Justice & Environmental Racism – Greenaction for Health and Environmental Justice," n.d. https://greenaction.org/what-is-environmental-justice/.
39. Suneson, Grant Usa Today. "What Are the 25 Lowest Paying Jobs in the US? Women Usually Hold Them." WLST, June 7, 2019. https://eu.usatoday.com/story/money/2019/04/04/25-lowest-paying-jobs-in-us-2019-includes-cooking-cleaning/39264277/.

40. Silva, Christianna. "Black Activist Burnout: 'You Can't Do This Work If You're Running On Empty.'" NPR.org, August 10, 2020. https://www.npr.org/2020/08/10/896695759/black-activist-burnout-you-can-t-do-this-work-if-you-re-running-on-empty.
41. Ujifusa, Andrew. "Rep. Marjorie Taylor Greene Barred From Spot on the Education Committee." Education Week, February 8, 2021. https://www.edweek.org/policy-politics/rep-marjorie-taylor-greene-barred-from-spot-on-the-education-committee/2021/02.
42. govinfo.gov. "Public Law 88-352," July 2, 1964. https://www.govinfo.gov/content/pkg/STATUTE-78/pdf/STATUTE-78-Pg241.pdf#page=1.
43. "The Origins of 'Antibusing' Politics: New York City Protests and Revision of the Civil Rights Act." The Gotham Center for New York City History, August 29, 2019. https://www.gothamcenter.org/blog/the-origins-of-antibusing-politics-new-york-city-protests-and-revision-of-the-civil-rights-act.
44. Data Team. "School Diversity in NYC," n.d. https://council.nyc.gov/data/school-diversity-in-nyc/.
45. Gould, Jessica, Jessica Gould, James Ramsay, Jake Offenhartz, Jake Offenhartz, David Cruz, Gwynne Hogan, and Gwynne Hogan. "New York's Schools Are Still The Most Segregated In The Nation: Report," June 11, 2021. https://gothamist.com/news/new-yorks-schools-are-still-the-most-segregated-in-the-nation-report.
46. Gould et al., "New York's Schools Are Still The Most Segregated In The Nation: Report," June 11, 2021.

BIBLIOGRAPHY

47. Shapiro, Eliza. "New York Schools Are Segregated. Will the Next Mayor Change That?" The New York Times, January 29, 2021. https://www.nytimes.com/2021/01/29/nyregion/nyc-mayoral-race-school-segregation.html.
48. Browne-Marshall, "Busing Ended 20 Years Ago. Today Our Schools Are Segregated Once Again," September 11, 2019.
49. Barnum, Matt. "Did Busing for School Integration Succeed? Here's What Research Says. - Chalkbeat: Essential Education Reporting across America." Chalkbeat, February 3, 2020. https://www.chalkbeat.org/2019/7/1/21121022/did-busing-for-school-desegregation-succeed-here-s-what-research-says.
50. Smith, Clint. "The Desegregation and Resegregation of Charlotte's Schools." The New Yorker, October 3, 2016. https://www.newyorker.com/news/news-desk/the-desegregation-and-resegregation-of-charlottes-schools.
51. Bowles, Nellie. "Kamala Harris and Classmates Were Bused Across Berkeley. The Experience Changed Them." The New York Times, July 1, 2019. https://www.nytimes.com/2019/06/30/us/politics/kamala-harris-berkeley-busing.html.
52. LII / Legal Information Institute. "Affirmative Action," n.d. https://www.law.cornell.edu/wex/affirmative_action.
53. Cmt Admin, "High School Jobs: Impact Is Different for Whites and Minorities," Institute for Social Research, n.d., https://isr.umich.edu/news-events/news-releases/high-school-jobs-impact-is-different-for-whites-and-minorities/

54. Justia Law. "Fisher v. University of Texas at Austin, 579 US ___ (2016)," n.d. https://supreme.justia.com/cases/federal/us/579/14-981/.
55. niea.org. "National Indian Education Association," n.d. https://www.niea.org/.
56. "Hispanic Scholarship Fund," n.d. https://www.hsf.net/.
57. Year Up. "Job Training to Close the Opportunity Divide," n.d. https://www.yearup.org/.
58. "UMass Boston," n.d. https://www.umb.edu/academics/vpass/aassp.
59. Nichols, Andrew Howard. "Graduation Rates Don't Tell the Full Story: Racial Gaps in College Success Are Larger Than We Think." The Education Trust, January 6, 2021. https://edtrust.org/resource/graduation-rates-dont-tell-the-full-story-racial-gaps-in-college-success-are-larger-than-we-think/.
60. Chen, Victor Tan. "The Lonely Poverty of America's White Working Class." The Atlantic, January 17, 2016. https://www.theatlantic.com/business/archive/2016/01/white-working-class-poverty/424341/.
61. "USDA ERS - Rural Employment and Unemployment," n.d. https://www.ers.usda.gov/topics/rural-economy-population/employment-education/rural-employment-and-unemployment/.
62. Gateway Foundation. "Substance Abuse in Rural Communities," August 25, 2021. https://www.gatewayfoundation.org/addiction-blog/rural-substance-abuse/.

63. BestColleges.com. "Rural Student College Attendance Takes a Dive | BestColleges," n.d. https://www.bestcolleges.com/blog/rural-students-college-enrollment-decline/.
64. The Moth. "The Moth | Education Program," n.d. https://themoth.org/education.
65. "Common Core State Standards |," n.d. http://www.corestandards.org/.
66. "Paul Robeson High School," n.d. https://robeson.philasd.org/.
67. "The Workshop School | Teaching Students to Change the World," n.d. https://www.workshopschool.org/.
68. Dalton, Shamika. "Minimizing and Addressing Implicit Bias in the Workplace: Be Proactive, Part One | Dalton | College & Research Libraries News," October 4, 2018. https://crln.acrl.org/index.php/crlnews/article/view/17370/19151.
69. Working on a warmer - international labour organization. (n.d.). https://www.ilo.org/wcmsp5/groups/public/---dgreports/---dcomm/---publ/documents/publication/wcms_711919.pdf
70. "Forrester Reprint," n.d. https://reprints2.forrester.com/.
71. Sundiatu Dixon-Fyle et al., "Diversity Wins: How Inclusion Matters," McKinsey & Company, December 9, 2022, https://www.mckinsey.com/featured-insights/diversity-and-inclusion/diversity-wins-how-inclusion-matters
72. Kellogg Insight. "Yes, Investors Care About Gender Diversity," February 22, 2021. https://insight.kellogg.northwestern.edu/article/women-in-tech-finance-gender-diversity-investors.

73. "Protected Characteristics | Equality and Human Rights Commission," n.d. https://www.equalityhumanrights.com/en/equality-act/protected-characteristics.
74. Steinpreis, Rhea. "The Impact of Gender on the Review of the Curricula Vitae of Job Applicants and Tenure Candidates: A National Empirical Study." SpringerLink, October 1, 1999. https://link.springer.com/article/10.1023/A:1018839203698?error=cookies_not_supported&code=d74d9458-f32c-465a-a3ac-cd7ff5bb440a.
75. CMS-Next POC. "Does Gender Bias Play a Role During an Interview?," n.d. https://www.monster.ca/career-advice/article/gender-role-during-a-job-interview-ca.
76. Holzwarth, Aline. "How To Actually Hire For Diversity." Forbes, February 18, 2021. https://www.forbes.com/sites/alineholzwarth/2021/02/18/how-to-actually-hire-for-diversity/?sh=2dcfc96e46f9.
77. Macan, Therese. "The Employment Interview: A Review of Current Studies and Directions for Future Research." Human Resource Management Review 19, no. 3 (September 2009): 203–18. https://doi.org/10.1016/j.hrmr.2009.03.006.
78. Chang, Edward H., Erika L. Kirgios, Aneesh Rai, and Katherine L. Milkman. "The Isolated Choice Effect and Its Implications for Gender Diversity in Organizations." Management Science 66, no. 6 (June 2020): 2752–61. https://doi.org/10.1287/mnsc.2019.3533.

BIBLIOGRAPHY

79. ACLU of Southern California. "Inclusion Targets: What's Legal?," February 26, 2019. https://www.aclusocal.org/en/inclusion-targets-whats-legal.
80. Allegis Group. "Unconscious Bias in the Workplace," January 3, 2020. https://www.allegisgroup.com/en-gb/insights/blog/2020/january/unconscious-bias-in-the-workplace.
81. Kaminsky, Michelle Esq. "Five Biggest Sexual Harassment Cases." LegalZoom, October 24, 2022. https://www.legalzoom.com/articles/five-biggest-sexual-harassment-cases.
82. "Mitsubishi Sustainability Report 2022," 2020. https://www.mitsubishielectric.com/en/sustainability/csr/social/labor/environment/index.html.
83. Fisher, Max, and Amanda Taub. "How Everyday Social Media Users Become Real-World Extremists." The New York Times, April 26, 2018. https://www.nytimes.com/2018/04/25/world/asia/facebook-extremism.html.
84. Shelly Tan, Youjin Shin. "How One of America's Ugliest Days Unraveled inside and Outside the Capitol." The Washington Post. WP Company, January 9, 2021. https://www.washingtonpost.com/nation/interactive/2021/capitol-insurrection-visual-timeline/.
85. Samuelson, Kate. "What to Know About Pizzagate, the Fake News Story With Real Consequences." Time, December 5, 2016. https://time.com/4590255/pizzagate-fake-news-what-to-know/.
86. "BlackLivesMatter," n.d. https://blacklivesmatter.com/.

87. https://www.hrc.org/. "The Human Rights Campaign," n.d. https://www.hrc.org/.
88. American Civil Liberties Union. "ACLU," December 8, 2022. https://www.aclu.org/.
89. Instagram. "@impact," n.d. https://www.instagram.com/impact/?hl=en.
90. Instagram. "@soyouwannatalkabout," n.d. https://www.instagram.com/soyouwannatalkabout/?hl=en.
91. Instagram. "Anti-Racism Daily," n.d. https://www.instagram.com/ardtakeaction/?hl=en.
92. Instagram. "What is Cash Bail? - ACLU." Accessed July 7, 2021. https://www.instagram.com/p/CR1uTsMsnDh/.
93. Instagram. "@ACLU_Nationwide," n.d. https://www.instagram.com/aclu_nationwide/?hl=en.
94. Desere Davis, Content Writer @ SocialPlanner.io. "Marketing Campaigns That Went Viral And Why They Were Awesome." SocialPlanner.io, November 1, 2020. https://socialplanner.io/blog/marketing-campaigns-that-went-viral-and-why-they-were-awesome/.
95. Sedonerrr, S. "It's 2021 and We Are Still Fighting for Bits and Pieces of Equality. #ncaa #inequality #fightforchange." TikTok, n.d. https://www.tiktok.com/@sedonerrr/video/6941180880127888646?sender_device=pc.
96. Twitter. "AJ McCord On," March 19, 2021. https://twitter.com/AJ_McCord/status/1372759106121912320.

BIBLIOGRAPHY

97. Congress.gov. "H.R.7120 - George Floyd Justice in Policing Act of 2020," n.d. https://www.congress.gov/bill/116th-congress/house-bill/7120.
98. "BlackLivesMatter," n.d. https://blacklivesmatter.com/.
99. "GoFundMe: #1 Fundraising Platform for Crowdfunding," n.d. https://www.gofundme.com/.
100. "Kickstarter," n.d. https://www.kickstarter.com/.
101. Indiegogo. "Crowdfund Innovations & Support Entrepreneurs," n.d. https://www.indiegogo.com/.
102. gofundme.com. "Tuition for FGLI Hispanic Student, Organized by Alondra Carmona," n.d. https://www.gofundme.com/f/tuition-for-fgli-hispanic-student.
103. gofundme.com. "LOVE ARMY FOR ROHINGYA, Organized by Jérôme Jarre," n.d. https://www.gofundme.com/f/love-army-for-rohingya.
104. gofundme.com. "DEI Mutual Aid Fund for BAM Staff, Organized by DEI Task Force," n.d. https://www.gofundme.com/f/dei-mutual-aid-fund-for-bam-staff.
105. gofundme.com. "Trans Women of Color Solidarity Network Fund, Organized by Trans Women of Color Solidarity Network," n.d. https://www.gofundme.com/f/trans-women-of-color-solidarity-network-fund.
106. gofundme.com. "TIME'S UP Legal Defense Fund, Organized by TIME'S UP Legal Defense Fund," n.d. https://www.gofundme.com/f/timesup.

107. gofundme.com. "Official George Floyd Memorial Fund, Organized by Philonise Floyd," n.d. https://www.gofundme.com/f/georgefloyd.
108. "NY Daily News," January 22, 2021. https://www.tribpub.com/gdpr/nydailynews.com/.
109. Monroe, Rachel. "GoFundMe Can Get Very Ugly." The Atlantic, January 20, 2021. https://www.theatlantic.com/magazine/archive/2019/11/gofundme-nation/598369/.
110. Nike.com. "Nike," n.d. https://www.nike.com/nl/.
111. Fly by Jing. "Fly By Jing," n.d. https://flybyjing.com.
112. Brex. "Brex Journal," n.d. https://www.brex.com/journal.
113. Techopedia. "Bootstrap." Techopedia.com, February 23, 2017. https://www.techopedia.com/definition/3328/bootstrap.
114. The story behind fly by Jing and cult favorite hot sauce, sichuan chili crisp. Here Magazine. (n.d.). https://www.heremagazine.com/articles/fly-by-jing-chengdu-china-interview
115. "What Is D2C and D2C Meaning: What Is Direct to Consumer?," n.d. https://www.bluecart.com/blog/d2c-meaning.
116. https://www.instagram.com/p/CHZB_wwhX0H/
117. The Coca-Cola Company. "The Coca-Cola Company: Refresh the World. Make a Difference," n.d. https://www.coca-colacompany.com/.
118. "Apple," n.d. https://www.apple.com/.
119. FS Investments. "Diversity + Inclusion," June 30, 2022. https://fsinvestments.com/company/diversity-inclusion/.
120. Bimbo Bakeries USA. "BimboBakeries," n.d. https://www.bimbobakeriesusa.com/.

BIBLIOGRAPHY

121. Kids, Coded By. "Coded by Kids," n.d. https://codedbykids.com/.
122. Hong, Lu, and Scott E. Page. "Groups of Diverse Problem Solvers Can Outperform Groups of High-Ability Problem Solvers." Proceedings of the National Academy of Sciences 101, no. 46 (November 8, 2004): 16385–89. https://doi.org/10.1073/pnas.0403723101.
123. Fry, R. (2021, April 1). Stem jobs see uneven progress in increasing gender, racial and ethnic diversity. Pew Research Center Science & Society. https://www.pewresearch.org/science/2021/04/01/stem-jobs-see-uneven-progress-in-increasing-gender-racial-and-ethnic-diversity/
124. "Modeling the Future Challenge – Real-World Actuarial Math Modeling Scholarship Competition for High School Students!," n.d. https://www.mtfchallenge.org/.
125. "TEAMS," n.d. https://tsaweb.org/teams.
126. Talaria ATHENA. "Talaria Summer Institute," n.d. https://talariasummerinstitute.org/.
127. Black Girls CODE. "BGC," November 19, 2022. https://wearebgc.org/.
128. "Multicultural Resource Center (MRC)— Office of the Vice Provost for Educational Equity," n.d. http://equity.psu.edu/mrc.
129. US Census Bureau. "Inequalities Persist Despite Decline in Poverty For All Major Race and Hispanic Origin Groups." Census.gov, December 9, 2021. https://www.census.gov/

library/stories/2020/09/poverty-rates-for-blacks-and-hispanics-reached-historic-lows-in-2019.html.
130. Jackson, Candace. "What Is Redlining?" The New York Times, August 17, 2021. https://www.nytimes.com/2021/08/17/realestate/what-is-redlining.html.
131. "Definition of Overpolice." In Www.Dictionary.Com, n.d. https://www.dictionary.com/browse/overpolice.
132. justice.gov. "Investigation of the Ferguson Police Department," March 4, 2015. https://www.justice.gov/sites/default/files/opa/press-releases/attachments/2015/03/04/ferguson_police_department_report.pdf.
133. Balko, Radley. "There's Racial Bias in Our Police Systems. Here's the Overwhelming Proof." Washington Post, June 11, 2020. https://www.washingtonpost.com/graphics/2020/opinions/systemic-racism-police-evidence-criminal-justice-system/.
134. Pierson E, Simoiu C, Overgoor J, Corbett-Davies S, Jenson D, Shoemaker A, Ramachandran V, Barghouty P, Phillips C, Shroff R, Goel S. A large-scale analysis of racial disparities in police stops across the United States. Nat Hum Behav. 2020 Jul;4(7):736-745. doi: 10.1038/s41562-020-0858-1. Epub 2020 May 4. PMID: 32367028.
135. ussc.gov. "Demographic Differences in Sentencing: An Update to the 2012 Booker Report," n.d. https://www.ussc.gov/sites/default/files/pdf/research-and-publications/research-publications/2017/20171114_Demographics.pdf.

136. Tsioulcas, Anastasia. "Some Are Calling the Buffalo Suspect a 'teenager.' Is That a Privilege of His Race?" NPR.org, May 16, 2022. https://www.npr.org/2022/05/16/1099137936/some-are-calling-the-buffalo-suspect-a-teenager-is-that-a-privilege-of-his-race.

137. Tompkins, Lucy. "Here's What You Need to Know About Elijah McClain's Death." The New York Times, January 19, 2022. https://www.nytimes.com/article/who-was-elijah-mcclain.html.

138. Tompkins, "Here's What You Need to Know About Elijah McClain's Death," January 19, 2022.

139. Lampen, Claire. "What We Know About the Killing of Elijah McClain." The Cut, September 1, 2021. https://www.thecut.com/2021/09/the-killing-of-elijah-mcclain-everything-we-know.html.

140. Jones, Julia. "Authorities Claimed These Black Men Had Excited Delirium Just before They Died. But the Diagnosis Itself Is a Problem and Should Be Abandoned, a New Study Says." CNN, March 12, 2022. https://edition.cnn.com/2022/03/12/us/excited-delirium-police-deaths-study/index.html.

141. Kovaleski, Jennifer. "Aurora Paramedics Gave Maximum Dose of Ketamine Even When Patient's Weight Was Unknown." Denver 7 Colorado News, October 2, 2020. https://www.denver7.com/news/investigations/aurora-paramedics-gave-maximum-dose-of-ketamine-even-when-patients-weight-was-unknown.

142. apa.org. "Black Boys Viewed as Older, Less Innocent Than Whites, Research Finds," 2014. https://www.apa.org/news/press/releases/2014/03/black-boys-older.
143. Wilson, John Paul, Kurt Hugenberg, and Nicholas O. Rule. "Racial Bias in Judgments of Physical Size and Formidability: From Size to Threat." Journal of Personality and Social Psychology 113, no. 1 (July 2017): 59–80. https://doi.org/10.1037/pspi0000092.
144. Asare, Janice Gassam, PhD. "4c Hair Discrimination: An Exploration Of Texturism," August 22, 2022. https://www.linkedin.com/pulse/4c-hair-discrimination-exploration-texturism-asare-ph-d-.
145. "Colorism." In The Merriam-Webster.Com Dictionary, n.d. https://www.merriam-webster.com/dictionary/colorism.
146. Behavior, Necessary. "The Natural Hair Movement: History, Stigma, and Successes." Necessary Behavior, May 5, 2021. https://www.necessarybehavior.com/blogs/news/the-natural-hair-movement-history-stigma-and-successes.
147. Blay, Zeba. "Let's Talk About Colorism In The Natural Hair Community." HuffPost, January 8, 2016. https://www.huffpost.com/entry/lets-talk-about-colorism-in-the-natural-hair-community_n_566df1dfe4b011b83a6ba4f0.
148. Rahman, Mahima. "Digital Commons Wayne State." https://digitalcommons.wayne.edu/cgi/viewcontent.cgi?article=1069&context=honorstheses, December 14, 2020. https://digitalcommons.wayne.edu/cgi/viewcontent.cgi?article=1069.

Bibliography

149. Congress.gov. "H.R.2116 - Creating a Respectful and Open World for Natural Hair Act of 2022," n.d. https://www.congress.gov/bill/117th-congress/house-bill/2116/text.

150. Gonzales, Matt. "CROWN Act: Does Your State Prohibit Hair Discrimination?" SHRM, August 19, 2022. https://www.shrm.org/resourcesandtools/hr-topics/behavioral-competencies/global-and-cultural-effectiveness/pages/crown-act-does-your-state-prohibit-hair-discrimination.aspx.

151. Jacobs, Julia, and Dan Levin. "Black Girl Sent Home From School Over Hair Extensions." The New York Times, August 22, 2018. https://www.nytimes.com/2018/08/21/us/black-student-extensions-louisiana.html.

152. Jacobs and Levin, "Black Girl Sent Home From School Over Hair Extensions."

153. "Black Women and Identity: What's Hair Got to Do With It?," n.d. https://quod.lib.umich.edu/cgi/t/text/text-idx?cc=mfsfront;c=mfs;c=mfsfront;idno=ark5583.0022.105;view=text;rgn=main;xc=1;g=mfsg.

154. AAFP. "Gun Violence, Prevention of (Position Paper)," n.d. https://www.aafp.org/about/policies/all/gun-violence.html.

155. Brennan Center for Justice. "Address Gun Violence by Going After the Root Causes," November 17, 2022. https://www.brennancenter.org/our-work/analysis-opinion/address-gun-violence-going-after-root-causes.

156. Frattaroli, Shannon. "Grassroots Advocacy for Gun Violence Prevention: A Status Report on Mobilizing a Movement."

Journal of Public Health Policy 24, no. 3/4 (2003): 332. https://doi.org/10.2307/3343381.

157. Walsh, Colleen. "Solving Racial Disparities in Policing." Harvard Gazette, February 24, 2021. https://news.harvard.edu/gazette/story/2021/02/solving-racial-disparities-in-policing/.

158. Bui, Quoctrung, Alicia Parlapiano, and Margot Sanger-Katz. "The Mass Shootings Where Stricter Gun Laws Might Have Made a Difference." The New York Times, June 5, 2022. https://www.nytimes.com/interactive/2022/06/04/upshot/mass-shooting-gun-laws.html.

159. Johns Hopkins Bloomberg School of Public Health. "Policies That Reduce Gun Violence: Firearm Purchaser Licensing," July 23, 2021. https://publichealth.jhu.edu/2021/policies-that-reduce-gun-violence-firearm-purchaser-licensing.

160. Morrison, Amanda, PhD. "What Is Ethnic Studies?" https://academicsenate.santarosa.edu/, n.d. https://academicsenate.santarosa.edu/sites/academicsenate.santarosa.edu/files/documents/A_Morrison_OPEN_FORUM_What+Is+Ethnic+Studies_07_22_2020.pdf.

161. Morrison, "What Is Ethnic Studies?"

162. Morrison, "What Is Ethnic Studies?"

163. https://www.diversifyournarrative.com/. "Diversify Our Narrative," n.d. https://www.diversifyournarrative.com/.

164. Diversity Our Narrative. "Lesson Plans," n.d. https://www.diversifyournarrative.com/lesson-plans?offset=1621230600096.

165. Diversity Our Narrative. "Our Chapters," n.d. https://www.diversifyournarrative.com/our-chapters.
166. Instagram. "@DiversifyOurNarrative," n.d. http://www.instagram.com/diversifyournarrative.
167. Nguyen, Terry. "Student Activists Want Their Schools to Adopt an Anti-Racist Education." Vox, July 29, 2020. https://www.vox.com/identities/2020/7/29/21345114/students-diversify-curriculum-change-antiracist.
168. Depenbrock, Julie. "Ethnic Studies: A Movement Born Of A Ban." NPR.org, August 13, 2017. https://www.npr.org/sections/ed/2017/08/13/541814668/ethnic-studies-a-movement-born-of-a-ban.
169. Yettick, Holly. "Academic Benefits of Mexican-American Studies Reaffirmed in New Analysis." Education Week, October 5, 2022. https://www.edweek.org/teaching-learning/academic-benefits-of-mexican-american-studies-reaffirmed-in-new-analysis/2014/11.
170. Depenbrock, "Ethnic Studies: A Movement Born Of A Ban," August 13, 2017.
171. Depenbrock, Julie, and Julie Depenbrock. "Federal Judge Finds Racism Behind Arizona Law Banning Ethnic Studies." NPR.org, August 23, 2017. https://www.npr.org/sections/ed/2017/08/22/545402866/federal-judge-finds-racism-behind-arizona-law-banning-ethnic-studies.
172. Learning for Justice. "The Fight for Ethnic Studies," n.d. https://www.learningforjustice.org/magazine/spring-2021/the-fight-for-ethnic-studies.

173. Sleeter, Christine, and Miguel Zavala. "WHAT THE RESEARCH SAYS ABOUT ETHNIC STUDIES." National Education Association, n.d. https://www.nea.org/sites/default/files/2020-10/What%20the%20Research%20Says%20About%20Ethnic%20Studies.pdf.
174. Depenbrock, Julie. "Ethnic Studies: A Movement Born Of A Ban." NPR.org, August 13, 2017.
175. Sleeter and Zavala, "WHAT THE RESEARCH SAYS ABOUT ETHNIC STUDIES."
176. Kai-Hwa Wang, Frances. "How Violence against Asian Americans Has Grown and How to Stop It, According to Activists." PBS NewsHour, April 11, 2022. https://www.pbs.org/newshour/nation/a-year-after-atlanta-and-indianapolis-shootings-targeting-asian-americans-activists-say-we-cant-lose-momentum.
177. Lee, Jennifer. "Confronting the Invisibility of Anti-Asian Racism." Brookings, May 18, 2022. https://www.brookings.edu/blog/how-we-rise/2022/05/18/confronting-the-invisibility-of-anti-asian-racism/.
178. NPR.org. "More Than 9,000 Anti-Asian Incidents Have Been Reported Since The Pandemic Began," August 13, 2021. https://www.npr.org/2021/08/12/1027236499/anti-asian-hate-crimes-assaults-pandemic-incidents-aapi.
179. "PROFILE | BTS | BIGHIT MUSIC," n.d. https://ibighit.com/bts/eng/profile/.
180. Orange County Register. "Here's How Boy Band BTS Inspired a School in South L.A. to Teach Korean Culture," October 14,

www.ingramcontent.com/pod-product-compliance
Lightning Source LLC
Chambersburg PA
CBHW020540030426
42337CB00013B/925